# OPTIONS TRADING CRASH COURSE

The No. 1 Beginner's Guide To Make Money With Trading Options In 10 Days Or Less.

**Logan Smith**

# Table Of Content

# Introduction

At the point amidst the vast majority of speculations to think of, you should consider purchasing stocks on the financial exchange (Options Trade), because many are most likely totally ignorant of terms like alternatives exchanging (Options Trading).

Purchasing stocks and clutching them with the end goal of making long haul gains, is all things considered, one of the more typical venture techniques. It's likewise an impeccably reasonable to way contribute, giving you have some thought regarding which stocks you ought to purchase or utilize a representative that can offer you exhortation and direction on such issues.

This methodology is known as an Option, holds procedure and can assist you with expanding your riches over the long haul, yet it doesn't give a lot, on the off chance that anything, in the method of transient additions. Nowadays, numerous financial specialists are deciding to utilize a progressively dynamic venture style so as to attempt to make increasingly prompt returns.

On account of the scope of online dealers that empower financial specialists to make exchanges on the stock trades with only a couple of snaps of their mouse, it's moderately clear for speculators to be progressively dynamic on the off chance that they wish to. There are numerous individuals that exchange online on either low maintenance or a full time premise; purchasing and selling normally to attempt to exploit shorter term value changes and regularly clutching their buys for only half a month or days, or even only two or three hours.

There are a lot of money related instruments that can be effectively exchanged. Alternatives, specifically have end up being well known among dealers and choices exchanging is turning out to be increasingly normal. In this book, we have given some valuable data on what is associated with alternatives exchanging and how it functions.

# Chapter One:
# Sojourning Into Options Trading

In extremely basic terms alternatives exchanging (Options Trading) includes purchasing and selling choices contracts on the open trades and, extensively, it's fundamentally the same as stock exchanging. While stock dealers plan to make benefits through purchasing stocks and selling them at a more significant expense, choices brokers can make benefits through purchasing alternatives agreements and selling them at a more significant expense. Likewise, similarly that stock brokers can take a short situation on stock that they accept will go down in esteem, choices merchants can do likewise with choices contracts.

Practically speaking be that as it may, this type of exchanging is definitely more flexible than stock exchanging. For a certain something, the way that alternatives agreements can be founded on wide assortment of hidden protections implies that there is a lot of extension with regards to choosing how and where to contribute. Brokers can utilize choices to conjecture on the value development of individual stocks, files, remote monetary forms, and items in addition to other things and this clearly presents undeniably more open doors for potential benefits.

The genuine adaptability, however, is in the different alternatives types that can be exchanged and the scope of various requests that can be put.

When exchanging stocks you essentially have two primary methods of bringing in cash, through taking either a long position or a short situation on a particular stock. In the event that you anticipated that a specific stock should go up in esteem, at that point you would take a long situation by purchasing that stock with the end goal of selling it later at a more significant expense. In the event that you anticipated that a specific stock should go down in esteem, at that point you would take a short situation by short offering that stock with a plan to repurchasing it later at a lower cost.

In choices exchanging, there's progressively decision in the manner in which exchanges can be executed and a lot more approaches to bring in cash.

It ought to be clarified that alternatives exchanging is a significantly more convoluted subject than stock exchanging and the entire idea of what is included can appear to be exceptionally overwhelming to apprentices. There is positively a ton you ought to learn before you really begin and put away your cash. All things considered, nonetheless, the greater part of the essentials aren't really that hard to grasp. When you have gotten a handle on the essentials, it turns out to be a lot more clear precisely what choices exchanging is about.

Beneath we clarify in more detail all the different procedures included.

**Purchasing Options**

Purchasing a choices contract is practically speaking indistinguishable to purchasing stock. You are fundamentally taking a long situation on that choice, anticipating that it should go up in esteem. You can purchase choices shrinks by just picking precisely what you wish to purchase and what number of, and afterward putting in a purchase to open request with a dealer. This request was named as such in light of the fact that you are opening a situation through purchasing choices.

In the event that your alternatives do go up in esteem, at that point you can either sell them or exercise your choice relying upon what suits you best. We give more data on selling and practicing alternatives later.

One of the huge points of interest of alternatives contracts is that you can get them in circumstances when you anticipate that the hidden resource should go up in esteem and furthermore in circumstances when you anticipate that the basic resource should go down.

On the off chance that you were anticipating that a basic resource should go up in esteem, at that point you would purchase call choices, which gives you the option to purchase the fundamental resource at a fixed cost. In the event that you were anticipating that a fundamental resource should go down in esteem, at that point you would purchase put choices, which gives you the option to sell the basic resource at a fixed cost. This is only one case of the adaptability on these agreements; there are a few more.

On the off chance that you have recently opened a short situation on choices decreases by keeping in touch with them, at that point you can likewise repurchase those agreements to close that position. To close a situation by purchasing contracts you would put in a purchase to close request with your agent.

**Selling and Writing Options**

There are essentially two manners by which you can sell choices contracts. To begin with, in the event that you have recently purchased agreements and wish to understand your benefits, or cut your misfortunes, at that point you would offer them by putting in an offer to close request. The request is named as such in light of the fact that you are shutting your situation by selling choices contracts.

You would for the most part utilize that request if the choices you possessed had gone up in worth and you needed to take your benefits by then, or if the choices you claimed had fallen in worth and you needed to leave your situation before causing some other misfortunes.

The other way you can sell choices is by opening a short position and short selling them. This is otherwise called composing choices, in light of the fact that the procedure really includes you composing new agreements to be sold in the market. At the point when you do this you are assuming the commitment in the agreement for example in the event that the holder decides to practice their alternative, at that point you would need to sell them the fundamental security at the strike cost (if a call choice) or purchase the basic security from them at the strike cost (if a put choice).

Composing alternatives is finished by utilizing the offer to open request, and you would get an installment at the hour of putting in such a request. This is commonly more hazardous than exchanging through purchasing and afterward selling, however there are benefits to be made on the off chance that you comprehend what you are doing. You would ordinarily submit such a request in the event that you accepted the important hidden security would not move so that the holder would have the option to practice their alternative for a benefit.

For instance, on the off chance that you accepted that a specific stock was going to either stay static or fall in esteem, at that point you could decide to compose and sell call choices dependent on that stock. You would be at risk to potential misfortunes if the stock went up in esteem, yet in the event that it neglected to do as such when the choices lapsed you would keep the installment you got for thinking of them.

**Practicing Options**

Choices brokers will in general make their benefits through the purchasing, selling, and composing of alternatives as opposed to ever really practicing them. Be that as it may, contingent upon the procedures you are utilizing and the reasons you have purchased certain agreements, there might be events when you decide to practice your choices to purchase or sell the hidden security.

The straightforward truth that you can conceivably bring in cash out of practicing just as purchasing and selling them further serves to outline exactly how much adaptability and flexibility this type of exchanging offers.

**Choices Spreads**

What truly makes exchanging alternatives such an intriguing method to contribute is the capacity to make choices spreads. You can unquestionably bring in cash exchanging by purchasing alternatives and afterward selling them on the off chance that you make a benefit, however the spreads are the genuinely useful assets in exchanging. A spread is basically when you enter a situation on at least two alternatives contracts dependent on the equivalent fundamental security; for instance, purchasing choices on a particular stock and furthermore composing agreements on a similar stock.

There are a wide range of sorts of spreads that you can make, and they can be utilized for a wide range of reasons. Most regularly, they are utilized as far as possible the hazard associated with taking a position or decreasing the money related expense required with taking a position. Most choices exchanging methodologies include the utilization of spreads. A few techniques can be extremely confused, yet there are likewise various genuinely fundamental systems that are straightforward.

**Advantages of Trading Options**

There are really various advantages this type of exchanging offers, in addition to the adaptability that we have alluded to above. It's proceeding to develop in prominence, with proficient brokers as well as with increasingly easygoing merchants too.

**WHAT ARE BINARY-OPTIONS THEMSELVES**

Twofold alternatives are straightforward choice agreement with a fixed hazard and fixed prize. These choices are called twofold alternatives in light of the fact that there is an "either decision" and an either payout after the choice lapses. Either decisions incorporate up or down, or contact and no/contact. In PC code parallel methods 1 or 0, or either.

The manner in which a parallel alternative works is from the merchants point of view (yours) is that you pick whether a specific fundamental resource (a stock, ware, money and so on) will go up or down in a specific measure of time. You basically wager cash on this forecast. You are shown how much cash in advance you will procure if your forecast is right. In the event that your forecast isn't right, you lose your wager and the cash gambled. In the event that you foresee accurately you recover your cash gambled PLUS an arrival. These profits normally are between 70-85%.

A short model would be that you anticipate the cost of gold to ascend from it's present cost of "$1612.75" one hour from now. The triumphant exchange offers an arrival of 80%. You place a $100 exchange on this thought.

One hour from now the choice agreement lapses (closes) and the agreement is evaluated as a "win" or a "misfortune", or "in the cash"/"out of the cash". Gold goes up to $1613, you anticipated effectively. You recover your $100 and an arrival of 80% – or $80 for a sum of $180. Despite the fact that gold just went up a minuscule sum, you despite everything gain the 80% return. Greatness of value development isn't a factor in the measure of your arrival.

**Key Ingredients Of A Binary Option Trade**

The entirety of the distinctive parallel choice agreements have these three key fixings that merchants need to observe. They are the expiry time, the strike cost, and the payout offers.

- Expiry Time

- Strike Price

- Payout Offer

The expiry time is essentially the time span from the second you 'purchase' the alternative agreement until it closes. This can be as quick as 60 seconds or up to a month. Most of brokers are exchanging the transient double choices, somewhere in the range of 60 seconds to 30 minutes.

The strike cost is the value that you had the option to enter the exchange at and this is the value that decides if your exchange is a champ or a washout. In the concise model over, the strike cost is

$1612.75. This is the value that gold expected to close at above so as to win this exchange.

The payout offer is the arrival that parallel choice agent is offering to you. In the gold exchange model over, the payout offer was 80% for a success and 0% for a misfortune. A few exchanges do have an arrival rate for misfortunes, commonly up to 10% in spite of the fact that this is dealer and exchange subordinate. The payout offer is known in advance before taking a chance with any cash.

**Kinds Of Binary Options Available**

There are different kinds of double alternatives accessible to exchange. The least complex and by a wide margin most basic exchange is the Up/Down exchange. You can find out about the various kinds of parallel choices accessible to exchange here.

**Novice Strategies**

We have arranged a rundown of essential double choice procedures that will assist you with beginning creation higher likelihood exchanges.

So now you comprehend the nuts and bolts of exchanging twofold choices. Some key things you ought to recollect before you make a plunge are these:

1. Your hazard is constrained to your exchange sum

2. The base exchange is as meager as $10

3. You do pay for losing exchanges – you lose your exchange sum (or most of it)

4. There is a lot of hazard included. Never at any point contribute more with a merchant than you can bear to lose. It's dangerous!

5. You never take any responsibility for basic resource – you just "wager" on its heading value development

6. To bring in cash over the drawn out you need to win most of your exchanges

7. Up/Down are just 1 sort of double alternative, there are a wide range of sorts of exchanges accessible to make with parallels

8. Exchanging double choices is intended to be anything but difficult to do.

Your hazard is restricted to the sum you place on the exchange. Your result is unmistakably expressed before making the exchange. On the off chance that you win a paired alternatives exchange you win a fixed measure of money. Since there are just two prospects, that is the beginning of the name "paired choices."

Choices exchanging can be intricate, considerably more so than stock exchanging. At the point when you purchase a stock, you choose what number of offers you need, and your representative takes care of the request at the overarching market cost or at a breaking point cost. Exchanging alternatives requires a portion of these components, yet additionally numerous others, including an increasingly broad procedure for opening a record.

**Opening Option exchanging account**

Before you can even begin you need to clear a couple of obstacles. On account of the measure of capital required and the unpredictability of anticipating various moving parts, merchants need to discover more about a potential financial specialist before granting them an authorization slip to begin exchanging alternatives.

Business firms screen potential alternatives merchants to survey their exchanging experience, their comprehension of the dangers in choices and their money related readiness.

**You'll have to give an imminent specialist:**

Venture destinations, for example, pay, development, capital conservation or theory

Exchanging experience, including your insight into contributing, to what extent you've been exchanging stocks or choices, what number of exchanges you make every year and the size of your exchanges

Individual budgetary data, including fluid total assets (or speculations handily sold for money), yearly pay, all out total assets and business data

**The kinds of alternatives you need to exchange**

In view of your answers, the specialist allocates you an underlying exchanging level (regularly 1 to 4, however a fifth level is getting increasingly normal) that is your vital aspect for putting particular kinds of choices exchanges.

Screening ought to go the two different ways. The agent you decide to exchange alternatives with is your most significant contributing accomplice. Finding the merchant that offers the devices, research, direction and bolster you need is particularly significant for financial specialists who are new to alternatives exchanging.

# Chapter Two:
# Center Elements In Options Trading

At the point when you take out an alternative, you're buying an agreement to purchase or sell a stock, typically 100 portions of the stock per contract, at a pre-arranged cost by a specific date. So as to put the exchange, you should settle on three vital decisions:

Choose which bearing you think the stock is going to move.

Foresee how high or low the stock cost will move from its present cost.

Decide the time span during which the stock is probably going to move.

1. Choose which course you think the stock is going to move

This figures out what sort of choices contract you take on. In the event that you think the cost of a stock will rise, you'll purchase a call choice. A call choice is an agreement that gives you the right, however not the commitment, to purchase a stock at a foreordained cost (called the strike cost) inside a specific timeframe.

In the event that you think the cost of a stock will decay, you'll purchase a put choice. A put alternative gives you the right, yet not the commitment, to sell shares at an expressed cost before the agreement lapses.

2. Foresee how high or low the stock cost will move from its present cost

A choice stays important just if the stock value shuts the alternative's termination period "in the cash." That implies either above or beneath the strike cost. (For call alternatives, it's over the strike; for put choices, it's underneath the strike.) You'll need to purchase a choice with a strike value that reflects where you anticipate the stock will be during the choice's lifetime.

For instance, in the event that you accept the offer cost of an organization at present exchanging for $100 is going to ascend to $120 by some future date, you'd purchase a call alternative with a strike cost under $120 (in a perfect world a strike value no higher than $120 less the expense of the choice, so the choice stays beneficial at $120). On the off chance that the stock does undoubtedly transcend the strike value, your alternative is in the cash.

So also, in the event that you accept the organization's offer cost is going to plunge to $80, you'd purchase a put choice (giving you the option to sell imparts) with a strike cost above $80 (in a perfect world a strike value no lower than $80 in addition to the expense of the choice, so the alternative stays gainful at $80). On the off chance that the stock dips under the strike value, your choice is in the cash.

You can't pick only any strike cost. Choice statements, in fact called alternative chains, contain a scope of accessible strike costs. The additions between strike costs are normalized over the business — for instance, $1, $2.50, $5, $10 — and depend on the stock cost.

The value you pay for an alternative, called the premium, has two segments: natural worth and time esteem. Natural worth is the distinction between the strike cost and the offer cost, if the stock cost is over the strike. Time esteem is anything that remains, and factors in how unpredictable the stock is, the opportunity to termination and financing costs, among different components. For instance, assume you have a $100 call choice while the stock expenses $110. How about we accept the choice's premium is $15. The inherent worth is $10 ($110 less $100), while time esteem is $5.

This leads us to the last decision you have to make before purchasing a choices contract.

3. Decide the time allotment during which the stock is probably going to move

Each choice agreement has a termination date that demonstrates the most recent day you can practice the choice. Here, as well, you can't simply haul a date out of nowhere. Your decisions are restricted to the ones offered when you call up a choice chain.

Termination dates can go from days to months to years. Every day and week by week choices will in general be the least secure and are saved for prepared choice dealers. For long haul financial specialists, month to month and yearly lapse dates are best. Longer terminations give the stock more opportunity to move and time for your venture theory to play out.

A more drawn out termination is additionally helpful in light of the fact that the alternative can hold time esteem, regardless of whether the stock exchanges underneath the strike cost. A choice's time esteem rots as lapse approaches, and choices purchasers would prefer not to watch their bought choices decrease in esteem, conceivably terminating useless if the stock completes underneath the strike cost. On the off chance that an exchange has conflicted with them, they can typically still sell whenever esteem staying on the choice — and this is almost certain if the alternative agreement is longer.

In the event that you think the cost of "Gold" is going up you place a "call".

On the off chance that you think the cost of "Gold" is going down, you place a "put".

Those are your solitary two alternatives. Subsequently "Double". In the event that you pick the correct decision of the two you win the exchange. On the off chance that you pick wrong you lose the exchange. There are two decisions in particular. 'Up or Down'. Furthermore, two results, 'Win or Lose'.

That is the very nuts and bolts of twofold exchanging for fakers. It is that straightforward, and it is intended to be that simple. Your arrival is obviously expressed before hitting the 'apply' button. You will acquire 72% on your venture in the event that you finish the exchange 'in the cash'.

"X" can be any number of basic resources. It tends to be a sure stock or it very well may be the cost of gold or oil. It very well may be a cash pair or it tends to be the cost of facebooks stock. You get the chance to pick what basic resource you need to exchange.

There is one progressively significant factor kept separate from the basic representation above and that is the termination time or development date of the alternative. This is the point in time when the exchange lapses. This is the moment that the genuine cost of the fundamental resource is resolved and you see whether you finish the exchange 'in the cash' with a success, or 'out of the cash' with a misfortune.

On the off chance that you picked 'up, or call' and at the cost lapsed higher, you win. The termination times shift from as quick as 60 seconds to as long as hours, days and even weeks.

Puts, calls, strike costs, premiums, subsidiaries, bear put spreads and bull call spreads — the language is only one of the intricate parts of alternatives exchanging. Be that as it may, don't let any of it drive you off.

Alternatives can give adaptability to financial specialists at each level and assist them with overseeing hazard. To check whether alternatives exchanging has a spot in your portfolio, here are the nuts and bolts of what choices are, the reason financial specialists use them and how to begin.

On further understanding, a choice is an agreement to purchase or sell a stock, typically 100 portions of the stock per contract, at a pre-arranged cost and by a specific date.

Similarly as you can purchase a stock since you figure the cost will go up or short a stock when you think its cost is going to drop, an alternative permits you to wager on which bearing you think the cost of a stock will go. Yet, rather than purchasing or shorting the advantage by and large, when you purchase a choice you're purchasing an agreement that permits — however doesn't commit — you to do various things, including:

Purchase or sell portions of a stock at a settled upon value (the "strike cost") for a constrained timeframe.

Offer the agreement to another financial specialist.

Let the alternative agreement lapse and leave moving along without any more money related commitment.

Choices exchanging may seem as though it's just for responsibility phobes, and it very well may be in case you're basically hoping to exploit momentary value developments and exchange and out of agreements — which we don't suggest. However, choices are helpful for long haul purchase and-hold financial specialists, as well.

**Why use Options?**

Financial specialists use choices for various reasons, yet the principle favorable circumstances are:

Purchasing a choice requires a littler starting expense than purchasing the stock. An alternative purchases a speculator time to perceive how things play out. A choice shields speculators from drawback hazard by securing in the cost without the commitment to purchase. In the event that there's an organization you've had your eye on and you accept the stock cost is going to rise, a "call" alternative gives you the option to buy shares at a predefined cost sometime in the future. In the event that your forecast works out you get the opportunity to purchase the stock for not as much as it's selling for on the open market. On the off chance that it doesn't, your money related misfortunes are constrained to the cost of the agreement.

You additionally can restrict your introduction to hazard on stock positions you as of now have. Suppose you own stock in an organization however are stressed over transient unpredictability clearing out your venture gains. To fence against misfortunes, you can purchase a "put" choice that gives you the option to sell a specific number of offers at a foreordained cost. On the off chance that the offer cost does to be sure tank, as far as possible your misfortunes, and the increases from selling help balance a portion of the monetary hurt.

**Step by step instructions to begin Options Trading**

So as to exchange alternatives, you'll need a representative. Look at our nitty gritty gathering of the best dealers for choices merchants, so you can analyze costs, essentials, and that's only the tip of the iceberg, just as our explainer on the most proficient method to open a money market fund. Or then again remain here and answer a couple of inquiries to get a customized proposal on the best specialist for your necessities.

In this article, you will find out about what choices are, the manner by which to purchase Put and Call alternatives, how to exchange choices and substantially more. On the off chance that Options Trading isn't for you, attempt our Harmonic Pattern Trading Strategy. It's a simple bit by bit control that has drawn a great deal of enthusiasm from perusers.

The Trading Strategy Guides group accepts this is the best alternatives procedure. When exchanging, we stick to the rule of KISS: "Keep it basic, Stupid!"

With effortlessness, our preferred position is having huge clearness over value activity.

We'll be concentrating on BUYING Put and Call choices through this choices exchanging instructional exercise. Selling alternatives is an alternate creature. It requires more understanding to completely comprehend the acquired dangers. Why? Since you can't control the drawback, a similar way you do when you purchase Put and Call choices.

This is the best choices system since it reliably gives productive exchange signals. Not on the grounds that it doesn't have misfortunes.

The favored time allotment best alternatives exchanging procedure is the brief time period.

We will initially characterize what purchasing a Put and Call alternatives is. From that point forward, we will give out the principles for the best alternatives exchanging procedure. Here is another system called The PPG Forex Trading Strategy.

Alternatives are a particular sort of subsidiaries contracts. The basic protections can be stocks, records, ETFs or items. With a subsidiaries contract, you don't legitimately claim the fundamental resource. Rather, you own a related resource whose worth is influenced by changes in cost.

With a choices contract, you reserve the privilege to purchase or sell a benefit at a foreordained cost later on. At the point when that future point shows up, you will have the decision to practice the alternative or let it terminate.

Here's a model. Suppose the advantage is selling for $110, an agreement giving you the option to purchase at $100 will have an inborn worth. As the termination date draws near, the estimation of the choices agreement will change.

There are two unique kinds of alternatives, call choices and put choices. At the point when utilized effectively, alternatives exchanging will make your technique considerably more unique. How about we plunge into the following area.

**CALL OPTION**

A Call Option gives you the option to buy a benefit later on. Whenever worked out, this buy will happen on a foreordained date. It will likewise happen at a foreordained worth. In the event that you are uncertain about the future estimation of an advantage, a call choice can offer some security. Call alternatives are usually bought by stock dealers. Be that as it may, they can likewise be found in numerous different markets. Truth be told, call alternatives are the most regularly exchanged choices contracts.

## PUT OPTION

A Put Option gives you the option to sell a benefit later on. Like call alternatives, these agreements have foreordained costs and sell dates. Put alternatives and assemble choices are regularly bought so as to make a "supported" position. Underneath, we will talk about the various kinds of choices deals. We will at that point talk about how these deals can be brought into your exchanging technique.

## KINDS OF OPTION SALES

It is important to recollect that a choice is an agreement that permits you to buy a benefit at a particular cost later on. There are four distinct sorts of choices deals that can happen. The contrasts among short and long deals, and puts and calls will be significant.

- A long call choice will give you the option to purchase a benefit at a particular cost later on. Long call choice holders will profit by cost increments after some time.

- A since quite a while ago put choice will give you the option to sell at a particular cost later on. As opposed to call alternatives, since quite a while ago put choice holders are trusting that market costs will diminish.

- A short call alternative gives you the option to sell not simply the fundamental resource, however the choice later on. Since the "rationale" of short positions is turned around, short call choice holders are in comparative situations to since a long time ago put alternative holders.

- A short put choice will trust that since quite a while ago put choices become less important after some time—thusly, holders will pull at costs to go up.

When you can comprehend the various assortments of choices deals, you will have the option to take part in progressively complex exchanging procedures. These procedures will as a rule include buying various choices so as to oversee hazard and increment the chance of gaining exceptional yields.

Alternatives are utilized for theory or supporting. Support investments directors are famous for utilizing propelled hazard the board techniques to fence their market introduction.

Choices offer high influence, allowing you to exchange huge agreements and conceivably get more cash-flow. This is the equivalent for Forex. You need a littler introductory speculation than purchasing stocks out and out. When purchasing choices, the hazard is constrained to the underlying premium cost paid.

When utilizing alternatives, the hazard is constrained, however the potential benefit is hypothetically boundless. Clearly, we state hypothetically boundless benefits. Be that as it may, choices costs will be extend bound inside specific parameters. There's no stock cost to ascend to interminability.

**TECHNIQUES OF OPTION TRADING**

You can take your exchanging past essential call and put choices. That is the excellence of choices exchanging. Other exchanging procedures incorporate secured call, wedded put, bull call spread, bear put spread, and the sky is the limit from there. They can assist you with bettering deal with your hazard and look for new exchanging chances.

In case you're an adaptable dealer, exploit the adaptability that alternatives exchanging can give you. Study the best 10 investment opportunities exchanging techniques beneath:

- Covered Call Strategy or purchase compose Strategy – suggests purchasing stocks by and large. Simultaneously, you need to sell call choices on a similar stock. The quantity of offers you purchased ought to be indistinguishable from the quantity of call choices contracts you sold.

- Married Put Strategy – suggests purchasing stocks by and large. Simultaneously, you will purchase put alternatives for a proportional number of offers. The wedded put works like a protection strategy against momentary misfortunes.

- Bull Call Spread Strategy – infers purchasing call choices with a particular strike cost. Simultaneously, you'll sell a similar number of call alternatives at a higher strike cost.

- Bear Put Spread Strategy – it's like the bull call spread yet includes purchasing and selling put choices. In this choices system, you purchase put choices with a particular strike cost. Simultaneously, sell a similar number of put choices at a lower strike cost.

- Protective Collar Strategy – suggests purchasing an out-of-the-cash put choice. Simultaneously sell or work an out-of-the-cash call alternative for a similar stock.

- Long Straddle Strategy – infers purchasing both a call alternative and a put choice simultaneously. The two choices ought to have a similar strike cost and termination date.

- Long Strangle Strategy – suggests purchasing both an out-of-the-cash call alternative and a put choice simultaneously. They have a similar lapse date however they have distinctive strike costs. The put strike cost will commonly be beneath the call strike cost.

- Butterfly Spread Strategy – suggests utilizing a mix of the bull spread methodology and bear spread technique. The old style butterfly spread includes getting one call choice at the most reduced strike cost. Simultaneously, sell two call choices at a higher strike cost. And afterward sell one final call choice at a considerably higher strike cost.

- Iron Condor Strategy – includes holding a long and a short situation in two distinctive choke systems.

- Iron Butterfly Strategy – includes utilizing a blend between either a long or short ride procedure. Simultaneously, purchase or sell a choke technique.

The main pointer required is RSI or Relative Strength Index.

Choices exchanging is obliged by the lapse date factor. So it's essential to choose a specialized marker that is reasonable for choices exchanging. The RSI pointer is an energy marker which makes it the ideal contender for choices exchanging. This is a direct result of its capacity to distinguish overbought and oversold conditions in the market.

The RSI pointer's area is on most FX exchanging stages (MT4, TradingView). You will discover it under the markers library.

All in all, how does the RSI marker truly work?

There is no compelling reason to go further into the math behind the RSI pointer. All we have to know is the manner by which to decipher the RSI wavering. Fundamentally, a RSI perusing equivalent to or beneath 30 shows that the market is in oversold conditions. A RSI understanding equivalent or over 70 shows the market is in overbought conditions. Simultaneously, a perusing over 50 is viewed as bullish. Then again, a perusing underneath 50 imprints is viewed as bearish.

The favored RSI pointer settings are the default settings with a 14 period.

**FRUITFUL RULES TO BUY CALL OPTIONS**

- **Options Trading Tutorial Step #1:** Wait 15-minutes after the financial exchange opens to build up your market inclination.

The best choices methodology isn't concentrating just on the cost. Be that as it may, they likewise utilize the time component equivalent to we're doing here.

The securities exchange opening cost is generally the most significant cost. During the principal minutes after the stock opening ringer, we can take note of a great deal of exchanging movement. This is on the grounds that that is when significant financial specialists are setting up their situations in the securities exchange.

Peruse Day Trading Price Action-Simple Price Action Strategy. You'll find out about a technique that isn't confined to the time component and spotlights on value activity. It's one of the most complete advisers for effectively exchange stocks or different resources by basically utilizing value activity.

Our group at Trading Strategy Guides needs to build up the best choices exchanging technique. So as to do that, we need to think more intelligent. We need to follow how the keen cash works in the market.

The best choices exchanging methodology won't keep you stuck to the screen throughout the day. You possibly need to know when the securities exchanges open.

The NYSE opens at 9:30 EST or 1:30 PM GMT time for those exchanging from Europe.

This gets us to the subsequent stage our choices exchanging instructional exercise...

- **Options Trading Tutorial Step #2:** Make sure the 15-Minute light after the initial ringer (9:30 EST) is bullish.

As we have built up before, we just need to exchange the heading where the savvy cash is. In case we're searching for purchasing Call Options opportunity we need to bring in sure shrewd cash is purchasing after the open. Then again, in case we're hoping to purchase Put Options we need to see venders show up directly after the initial chime.

Significant Note*: If we have an initial hole up it implies the purchasing power is considerably more grounded and we should put more weight on this exchange arrangement.

- **Options Trading Tutorial Step #3:** Check if the RSI is over 50 level – This is a bullish force signal.

We utilize the RSI marker for affirmation reason as it were. We need to ensure that once we have recognized the bullish value activity the force behind the move is affirmed by the RSI marker. We're not worried about overbought and oversold conditions in light of the fact that the market can remain in these conditions longer than you can remain dissolvable.

Presently, how about we hop and characterize where precisely we need to enter our purchase a Call choice.

- **Options Trading Tutorial Step #4:** Buy a Call alternative right at the opening of the second 15-minute flame after the initial ringer.

Presently, that we have affirmation that keen cash is purchasing we would prefer not to lose any additional time and we need to purchase a Call alternative right at the opening of the following 15-minute flame after the initial ringer.

As simple as it sounds this system just expects you to put 15-minutes of your time every day. You'll either get a sign or not, yet so as to exploit the best alternatives exchanging procedure, you have to practice discipline and don't take any exchanges in the event that you don't have any sign.

So now, our exchange is running and in benefit, however we despite everything need to characterize when to practice our call alternative and take benefit.

- **Options Trading Tutorial Step #5:** Choose the closest termination cycle. For day exchanging pick the week after week cycle.

At the point when you purchase a Call alternative you likewise need to settle a termination date, as a major aspect of that agreement.

You may be asking yourself how to pick the correct lapse cycle?

All things considered, in light of the fact that we're undoubtedly going to sell our Call choice a similar day as we have bought it, it's increasingly fitting to pick the week after week cycle.

Time to change our concentration to the most significant part: Where to take PROFITS and sell your Call Options?

- **Options Trading Tutorial Step #6:** Take Profit and sell the Call Option when you have two back to back 15-minute bearish candles.

Realizing when to take benefit is as significant as realizing when to enter an exchange. We need to escape our situation when we see the dealers stepping in. We measure this by checking two successive bearish candles as an indication of bearish opinion nearness in the market.

You would prefer not to practice your long Call alternative since you would prefer not to possess those offer stocks, you simply need to make a speedy benefit.

We've applied a similar Step #1 through Step#4 to assist us with building up our exchanging predisposition and distinguish the Buy Put Option exchange and finished Step #5 Step#6 to recognize when to sell your Call alternative.

**Choosing the Options Contract that is Right for You**

Since you see how to effectively exchange alternatives, you will need to realize how to pick the agreements that are directly for you. All choices agreements will have some level of hazard. This is particularly evident when exchanging twofold alternatives. This is because of the way that alternatives can conceivably be useless on their termination date. The danger of exchanging alternatives can be overseen.

While choosing alternatives, remember the accompanying things:

- Your own degree of hazard resistance

- Your ideal exchanging time allotment (day exchanging, long haul exchanging)

- The unpredictability of each planned resource

- Past profits for alternatives contracts

Choices contracts additionally have significant levels of suggested unpredictability. During the initial 30 minutes of exchanging, alternatives contracts experience enormous changes in esteem. At the point when unpredictability is high, both the degree of hazard and potential prize will be higher. During this time, your exchanging procedure should be significantly more dynamic. Hazard can be overseen by giving stop orders. It can likewise be overseen by supporting your position and differentiating your positions.

Both call and put choices can be fulfilling. So as to get ready yourself as an alternatives merchant, it will be a smart thought to rehearse. Luckily, Trading Strategy Guides makes it simple to sharpen your aptitudes and enter new markets. Cautiously consolidating the means referenced above can assist you with opening the best alternatives exchanging methodology.

This is one of the best choices systems since when exchanging stocks, it's critical to have a decent comprehension of the market assumption and how the large players are situated in the market. Another significant motivation behind why this is the best choices exchanging methodology is that you're not required to be stuck to the screen throughout the day.

# Chapter Three:
# Points Of Interest Of Option Trading

It's straightforward why purchasing stocks or exchanging them is engaging such a large number of financial specialists; it's generally easy to do and there is certainly cash to be made. Exchanging other money related instruments is regularly increasingly convoluted and this is presumably why numerous financial specialists and merchants do adhere to stocks. Notwithstanding, a portion of these other budgetary instruments can give different advantages that stocks don't.

Alternatives exchanging, specifically, has numerous focal points and there are a lot of reasons why this type of exchanging is deserving of thought for anybody hoping to contribute. On this page we take a gander at the primary purposes behind exchanging choices and why it very well may be such a smart thought, regardless of whether it is an increasingly perplexing subject with such a long way to go. The accompanying points are secured:

1. Capital Outlay and Cost Efficiency

2. Hazard and Reward

3. Adaptability and Versatility

## 1. Capital Outlay and Cost Efficiency

Perhaps the best explanation behind exchanging alternatives is the way that it's conceivable to make noteworthy benefits out of doing as such without essentially needing enormous aggregates of cash. Along these lines, it's optimal for financial specialists with small beginning capital just as those with bigger spending plans. The potential for huge benefits from little ventures is to a great extent down to the utilization of influence. In extremely basic terms, you can utilize influence to get all the more exchanging power from the capital you have.

For instance, suppose you had $1,000 to contribute and you wished to put it in Company X stock, at present exchanging at $20, which you expected to ascend in esteem. On the off chance that you decided to just purchase those stocks utilizing your $1,000, at that point you could buy 50 offers. In the event that the stock rose to, state, $25 then you would make a benefit of $5 per share for an aggregate of $250. This speaks to a 25% profit for your unique venture.

On the other hand, you could decide to purchase call choices on a similar stock, giving you the option to buy the stock. In the event that call choices with a strike cost of $20 were exchanging at $2.00 every, you could purchase 500 choices which would empower you to purchase 500 offers if the stock went up. With the stock ascending to $25, you could practice your choice to purchase 500 offers, and afterward sell them promptly for a benefit of $2,500.

Subsequent to removing your unique speculation of $1,000 to purchase the alternatives, you are still left with $1,500 benefit and an arrival on your cash of 150%.

This is a to some degree streamlined model, yet it illustrates how you can produce sizable comes back from whatever beginning capital you have accessible. This is an unmistakable bit of leeway that exchanging alternatives has over exchanging for all intents and purposes some other sort of money related instrument. Simply, you can set aside cash when taking a specific situation on the significant fundamental security which empowers you to make extremely cost productive ventures and exchanges. There are even various systems that can be utilized explicitly to diminish the expense of taking certain positions.

## 2. Hazard and Reward

In certain regards, the hazard versus reward advantage offered by exchanging alternatives is firmly connected to the above point. As the given model appeared, it's conceivable to make proportionately greater comes back from a similar capital venture. We utilized this guide to feature that exchanging should be possible with generally limited quantities of beginning capital and it very well may be an extremely cost effective approach to contribute. Furthermore, choices exchanging can offer a greatly improved hazard versus reward proportion if the correct exchanging methodologies are utilized.

It ought to be clarified that there are clearly chances included, in light of the fact that there are with a speculation. Some exchanging systems can be extremely unsafe in fact, particularly those that are exceptionally theoretical in nature. The general standard is that the higher the potential return, the higher the degree of hazard included. What is especially incredible, however, is the way that you can practically pick whatever degree of hazard you wish to take and exchange as needs be.

The wide scope of various alternatives gets that you can exchange and the various requests you can put make it a lot simpler to restrain hazard than it is when just purchasing and selling stocks. As you get familiar with choices and the manner in which they are exchanged, you will acknowledge exactly how ground-breaking an instrument they can be with regards to overseeing hazard.

## 3. Adaptability and Versatility

One of the most engaging components of choices is the adaptability that they offer. This is in agreement to most types of detached venture, and even some progressively dynamic structures, where there are restricted methodologies included and constrained approaches to bring in cash.

For instance, on the off chance that you are adopting a purchase and hold strategy to speculation and just purchasing stocks to construct a portfolio as long as possible, there are basically just two primary systems you can utilize. You can concentrate on long haul development and purchase the stocks that ought to acknowledge in an incentive after some time, or you can look for increasingly ordinary returns and purchase stocks that should offer standard profit pay outs.

Obviously, you can utilize a mix of the two and there are a couple of minor departure from the two principle methodologies, for example, regardless of whether to make safe speculations that include next to no hazard yet a constrained return or whether to face more challenge for incredible potential benefits. In any case, the truth of the matter is that there isn't generally an immense measure of degree for utilizing propelled methodologies to expand your degree of benefits.

Regardless of whether you are effectively exchanging stocks, there are sure impediments included. In exceptionally fundamental terms, you can either purchase stocks that you think will go up in worth or short sell stocks that you think will go down in esteem. There's absolutely a greater scope of systems that can be utilized when adopting the purchase and hold strategy, and various techniques that can be utilized to figure out what exchanges to make and when. Notwithstanding, the adaptability and flexibility in alternatives exchanging implies that you will discover many, a lot more open doors for making benefits in any predominant economic situation.

For a certain something, alternatives can be purchased and sold dependent on a wide assortment of hidden resources. Just as theorizing on the value developments of stocks, you can likewise estimate on value developments of files, products, and outside monetary forms. This reality alone methods there are an immense number of recognizable open doors for conceivably gainful exchanges.

For instance, you may have a specific ability for anticipating changes in the forex (remote trade) showcase just as a strong crucial information on a particular industry. You could utilize your expertise in the forex market to exchange alternatives dependent on remote monetary standards and furthermore utilize your industry information to exchange choices dependent on significant stocks. The potential for finding appropriate exchanges is practically boundless.

The scope of genuine exchanging techniques that can be utilized is likewise tremendous. Specifically, spreads offer genuine adaptability in the manner in which you exchange. Regardless of whether you are hoping to confine the danger of taking a position, lessen the forthright expense of taking that position, or endeavor to benefit from value developments in more than one course, it's spreads that make for genuine adaptability. They can likewise be utilized for supporting existing positions, which can be extremely helpful in dubious occasions. It's additionally conceivable to utilize alternatives spreads to benefit from a stale market, something that is troublesome when exchanging stocks.

**DISSERVICES OF OPTION TRADING**

It's genuinely simple to perceive any reason why exchanging choices is getting progressively well known among numerous financial specialists. It's not, at this point only the experts that are included, in light of the fact that an ever increasing number of easygoing financial specialists and home brokers are exploiting the advantages on offer. It isn't without its detriments however.

Most would agree that acing choices exchanging is no basic undertaking, and there is unquestionably a long way to go. This is surely the single main motivation why it's despite everything kept away from by such a significant number of, as the complexities of the subject can appear to be overpowering or in any event, threatening. It's absolutely a significant drawback that it's only not as clear the same number of different types of speculation. The benefits are there to be made. be that as it may, it takes a ton of time and duty to figure out how.

Another hindrance is the dangers in question. While there are hazards in any type of venture, exchanging choices can be especially dangerous, particularly for relative tenderfoots who don't have a colossal measure of understanding. The very idea of choices implies that they can be utilized to restrict chance, on the off chance that you comprehend the systems required, yet this type of exchanging shouldn't be considered as hazard free using any and all means.

## DANGERS INVOLVED WITH OPTIONS TRADING

In first experience with alternatives exchanging we have just given a point by point clarification of what choices are and what exchanging them involves, alongside a diagram of the considerable number of preferences. On the off chance that you are truly thinking about this type of exchanging as part, or all, of your venture methodology, at that point these essential subjects are imperative to know.

It's additionally fitting that, before you really begin, you likewise see a portion of the drawbacks to exchanging alternatives and the dangers in question.

With any type of contributing, your capital is at last in danger somewhat when you contribute it, and alternatives exchanging is the same. While there various ways that you can restrict your hazard, through utilizing the suitable exchanging procedures for instance, there are sure immediate and roundabout dangers that you should know about. On this page, we give further subtleties on this, covering the accompanying:

1. Potential Losses

2. Complexities

3. Liquidity

4. Expenses

5. Time Decay

### 1. Potential Losses in Options Trading

One of the numerous reasons that speculators decide to exchange alternatives is because of the adaptability and flexibility they offer, and the wide scope of systems that can be utilized. Specifically, there are various systems that can be utilized as far as possible the danger of taking a position or diminish the forthright expenses of taking a position.

With a portion of the constrained hazard procedures, it's conceivable to enter an exchange and know precisely what the greatest potential misfortune is, which can be exceptionally valuable when arranging exchanges. In any case, alternatives exchanging is generally viewed as high hazard and it's positively conceivable to make critical misfortunes. Clearly, the more you learn and the more experience you get the more outlandish you are to make calamitous misfortunes, however even experienced brokers can commit errors and it's imperative to recognize what kind of dangers you are presented to.

A significant bit of leeway that is frequently referenced is the way that you can utilize influence to adequately duplicate the intensity of your capital. For instance, on the off chance that you purchased $1,000 worth of call alternatives dependent on Company X stock then you could remain to make a lot greater benefits. On the off chance that that stock went up, at that point you ought to straightforwardly put that $1,000 into the stock.

Nonetheless, the other side to this is if the stock fell in esteem, or even just continued as before, your call alternatives may wind up useless and you would lose your whole $1,000. Had you purchased the stock rather, you would possibly lose all that $1,000 if Company X failed. This features a significant hazard, that it's feasible for alternatives that you purchase to lapse useless, which means you lose anything you put resources into those agreements.

Similarly, when composing choices, you can lose huge aggregates of cash if the hidden security moves significantly in cost in an ominous bearing. There are steps that you can take to confine misfortunes, for example, utilizing stop misfortune arranges or making spreads, however it's indispensable that you know about the potential misfortunes that you can cause in the case of purchasing agreements or keeping in touch with them.

## 2. Complexities of Options Trading

The very idea of choices exchanging and the complexities included is a hazard in itself. While it isn't generally that hard to comprehend the nuts and bolts, a few parts of alternatives exchanging and the techniques you can utilize are significantly increasingly convoluted. It's a genuinely regular mix-up for financial specialists, and especially fledglings, to not completely comprehend what they are doing and this can be a very risky slip-up to make.

You can beat this hazard by learning however much as could be expected, including the propelled subjects, and just utilizing techniques that you are totally acquainted with. It's very simple to re-think what you are doing and why, and this is something you should attempt to stay away from. Information will give you certainty.

### 3. Liquidity of Options

Choices exchanging is unmistakably more typical than it used to be, with an expanding number of speculators getting included, however there can even now be a few issues with liquidity of specific alternatives. Since there are such huge numbers of various sorts, it's very conceivable that a specific choice you wish to exchange may just be exchanged low volume.

This can introduce an issue, since it might make it hard to make the necessary exchanges at the correct costs. Is anything but a significant issue on the off chance that you are exchanging extremely little volumes or just exchanging the most well known choices, yet for those exchanging huge volumes or less standard choices it can make extra hazard. The trades normally use advertise creators to guarantee certain degrees of liquidity, however this doesn't really expel the issue.

### 4. Expenses of Trading Options

Firmly connected to the liquidity of certain alternatives is the costs engaged with exchanging them. The cost of a choices contract is constantly cited on the trades with an offer cost and an ask cost. The offer cost is the value you get for thinking of them and the ask cost is the value you pay for getting them.

The ask cost is consistently higher than the offered cost, and the contrast between these two costs is known as the offer ask spread, or the spread. The spread is fundamentally a roundabout expense of exchanging choices, and the greater the spread the more those costs increment. An absence of liquidity will for the most part lead to greater spreads, and this is another possibly critical hazard.

The immediate expenses of exchanging choices can likewise be higher than some different types of speculation: explicitly the commissions charged by representatives. Such costs are an unavoidable piece of any sort of speculation, and ought to consistently be calculated into any exchanging arrangement you get ready. The explanation they are especially pertinent to alternatives exchanging is that most systems include making spreads.

Making an alternatives spread includes entering at least two situations on various choices that depend on the equivalent fundamental security. There are excellent purposes behind making these spreads, yet the truth of the matter is that taking different positions adequately on a solitary exchange results in higher commissions.

## 5. Time Decay

Another unavoidable hazard is the impact of time rot. All alternatives have a period esteem calculated in to them, and ordinarily the more they have until termination the higher that time esteem is. Accordingly, any alternatives that you own will consistently be losing a portion of their incentive over the long haul. Obviously, this doesn't imply that they generally go down in esteem, yet time rot can contrarily affect the estimation of any choices that you clutch.

There are a few financial specialists that know about the dangers associated with exchanging alternatives and as a result of this they choose to keep away from choices as venture vehicle. The straightforward certainty is that it isn't for everybody; it's a generally remarkable approach to contribute and there are sure entanglements and drawbacks.

Nonetheless, no type of venture is without its hindrances and there are additionally a lot of reasons why exchanging alternatives is a smart thought. There are positively numerous financial specialists who do earn substantial sums of money from it and it's superbly feasible for anybody to do as such. On the off chance that you are thinking about getting included, at that point your choice should be founded on whether the benefits of exchanging alternatives exceeds the dangers associated with your view.

In the event that you do feel that exchanging choices is for you, at that point the following thing you coherently need to know is the place you can purchase, sell, and compose alternatives.

# Chapter Four: Where To Trade Options

One of the main things you have to arrange for when you are preparing to exchange alternatives is actually how you are going to make your exchanges for example where will you purchase, sell, and compose alternatives. Most alternatives contracts are purchased and sold on different choices trades based the world over. These trades are effectively available to the overall population, however you can't really complete the exchanges yourself. Similarly you need the administrations of a stock dealer to purchase and sell stocks on the world's stock trades, you need an agent to purchase and sell choices.

On this page we clarify somewhat more about utilizing agents to exchange choices. We additionally take a gander at the two fundamental manners by which representatives can be characterized: full help or markdown, and on the web or disconnected.

## UTILIZING A BROKER TO TRADE OPTIONS

Most stock intermediaries will complete choices exchanges for your sake, and there are likewise master choices agents who center explicitly around this specific budgetary instrument. Utilizing a merchant to exchange choices is exceptionally basic: you simply need to train them concerning what exchange you wish to complete and they will execute the exchange for you. Consequently, they will charge you a commission for every exchange, generally dependent on the size of the exchange in question.

There is a scope of various requests you can put with a representative, and these requests can be utilized to purchase contracts, sell existing agreements that you effectively own, and compose new agreements to sell. There are additionally sure specifications you can make as a major aspect of your requests, for example, least or most extreme costs to exchange at.

Picking an agent to use for exchanging alternatives can really be a troublesome choice, on the grounds that there are such a significant number of them. On the off chance that you as of now make ventures, in stocks and offers for instance, at that point you as of now have a record with an agent that can likewise be utilized to exchange alternatives. On the other hand, on the off chance that you have companions or relatives that you know utilize a dealer then you may wish to approach them for a suggestion.

**TWO MAIN TYPES OF BROKERS**

The two principle sorts of representatives are full help agents and markdown intermediaries. The contrasts between the two are basically in the administrations that they offer and the expenses and commissions that they charge. Full assistance agents are normally the more costly of the two, since you will have an individual contact that will work with you on your speculations.

A decent full assistance specialist will set aside the effort to comprehend your own conditions and your speculation destinations, and afterward offer counsel and direction on what ventures you ought to make. Through a mix of recognizing what you are attempting to accomplish and their own insight and aptitude, they ought to have the option to assist you with arriving at your speculation objectives.

As you can envision, you do pay a premium for this degree of administration. On the off chance that you utilize a full assistance merchant, at that point you will typically pay genuinely high commissions on the entirety of your exchanges, and you might be dependent upon month to month or yearly charges as well.

Rebate merchants, as the name proposes, are generally less expensive and they offer limited commissions and charges. You will commonly pay fundamentally less commission for every exchange that you make and different expenses will be kept to a base. In any case, you won't advantage from having an expert help you with your speculations. A rebate intermediary is basically there to take your requests and execute them as needs be.

On the off chance that you have next to no speculation experience, at that point the benefits of a full help agent are genuinely clear. Be that as it may, the additional costs included shouldn't be disregarded. In the event that you are exchanging with generally small beginning capital, at that point utilizing a full assistance intermediary could genuinely affect upon your benefits. Likewise, on the off chance that you plan on being sensibly dynamic in your choices exchanging, at that point it may not be reasonable to look for exhortation before each exchange that you can make and, obviously, the more exchanges you are having the more effect the higher commissions will have.

As an exceptionally broad standard, we would prompt that rebate representatives are the better decision for choices dealers.

## ONLINE BROKERS AND OFFLINE BROKERS

Before, a financial specialist's relationship with their dealer would for the most part have been a generally close to home one. It was very typical for financial specialists, especially ordinary speculators, and their agents to realize each other sensibly well. The most well-known path for speculators to put orders with their representative would be via phone, and there was a lot of individual collaboration. While there are numerous speculators nowadays that despite everything have such associations with their dealers, the utilization of online agents is getting progressively far reaching.

Online intermediaries are commonly rebate specialists, so on the off chance that you would like to utilize a full help intermediary you might be in an ideal situation utilizing a disconnected representative that you can converse with via phone. Be that as it may, on the off chance that keeping expenses and commissions low is a need for you, at that point an online dealer is very likely the best decision for you.

For most choices dealers, we would recommend that utilizing an online specialist is a lot of the best approach, for various reasons.

The primary explanation we have just referenced; the cost investment funds can be very considerable when utilizing an online intermediary since you will regularly pay significantly less commission on every exchange you make. There will commonly be less to pay in the method of other record expenses as well, except if you explicitly need access to the different devices and extra administrations that some online representatives make accessible at an expense. The subsequent explanation is the simplicity of making exchanges. Utilizing an online specialist is fantastically basic once you become accustomed to the exchanging stage, and submitting choices requests is ordinarily simply an issue of making a couple of snaps of the mouse.

On the off chance that you will be generally dynamic when exchanging alternatives, at that point the capacity to put arranges rapidly is an immense preferred position. In the event that you are utilizing a day exchanging style, at that point a couple of moments contrast in getting your requests set and executed can now and then be the distinction between bringing in cash on an exchange and losing cash. Regardless of whether you aren't especially dynamic and just exchange periodically, the upsides of utilizing an online specialist presumably settle on this a superior decision than utilizing a disconnected intermediary.

**BEST OPTION BROKERS FOR BEGINNERS**

Picking which intermediary to utilize when exchanging choices is without question one of the absolute most significant choices you will ever need to make in your exchanging profession. Utilizing a decent representative can set aside you cash, increment your productivity, spare you time, assist you with discovering exchanging openings, and it will for the most part improve your general exchanging experience.

Regardless of the significance of picking a specialist cautiously, numerous merchants join with any old intermediary and basically join the first they go over or the one that offers the best sign up impetus.

Not placing any idea into what intermediary to utilize is a serious mix-up in light of the fact that, this truly is a choice that is well worth investing some energy in.

In the event that you are sufficiently fortunate to know an accomplished merchant that you confide in then asking them which intermediary they use is a decent method to locate a conventional agent, yet that isn't a strategy that is accessible to everybody. Then again, you could evaluate a scope of various intermediaries, look at them, and choose which one is best for you. In any case, this would be pretty tedious.

A choice is an agreement that permits (however doesn't require) a financial specialist to purchase or sell a basic instrument like a security, ETF or file at a specific cost over a specific timeframe.

**HOW BROKERS ARE RANKED**

In the first place, we ought to likely clarify that there isn't generally any such thing as the "right" specialist from a general perspective. Choices merchants all have marginally various situations and somewhat various necessities and at last a ton is down to individual decision. A representative that is a decent decision for one dealer may not really be a decent decision for another merchant.

All things considered, we could never prescribe only one single representative to a wide crowd, however would prefer to furnish our perusers with a scope of recommendations and offer guidance on the most proficient method to choose the most appropriate. This is the reason we have grouped our suggestions into various classes.

**SIGNIFICANT FACTORS TO CONSIDER BEFORE OPTIONS TRADING**

While picking an intermediary you have to ponder which parts of an agent you should be mulling over. For tenderfoots and those hoping to make generally little exchanges, we accept that the accompanying components are especially significant and it's these that we propose you take a gander at when choosing which online choices representative to choose.

1. Full Service or Discount?

2. Commissions and Fees

3. Least Deposit and Minimum Trade Value

## 1. Full Service or Discount?

Generally, intermediaries could undoubtedly be put in one of two classes; they were either full assistance or markdown. The approach of online agents has made it fairly progressively hard to recognize the two as there will in general be much greater adaptability in the administrations advertised. Carefully, a full assistance specialist is one that will furnish you with proficient counsel and direction notwithstanding executing your requests for you while a rebate intermediary will essentially complete your requests as trained.

Nowadays various dealers can adequately be put in either, or both, of the classes as they offer a decision of administration to their clients. What you should choose is whether you need the extra administrations that are on offer, for example, accepting master guidance on potential exchanges and ventures, or whether you like to have a merchant that basically follows up on your guidelines. It won't shock you to realize that utilizing the extra administrations is the more costly alternative, and you will pay considerably less in commissions and charges when utilizing rebate administrations.

There's a thought coasting around that recommends apprentices are in an ideal situation utilizing a full assistance representative while they are as yet taking in and profiting by having an expert guide them as important. There are absolutely benefits in that game-plan, anyway we recommend that even apprentice choices brokers should utilize a markdown administration.

On the off chance that an alternate type of speculation was included, for example, putting resources into stocks and offers utilizing a purchase and hold technique, at that point the contentions for utilizing a full assistance agent would be more grounded in light of the fact that there are genuine advantages in having a specialist help you to design your ventures, find reasonable venture openings, and screen your portfolio.

In any case, choices exchanging is a special type of exchanging and there is quite a lot more required than just choosing stocks that will go up in an incentive in the long haul. As we would like to think, it's vastly improved to be hands on from the earliest starting point, figuring out how to distinguish your own exchanging openings, and choose which alternatives exchanging procedures to utilize.

Thusly, we would encourage novice merchants to adhere to limit benefits essentially for the reasons recorded above, yet additionally due to the extra costs engaged with utilizing a full help agent. The higher commission charges can truly eat into any profits that you make, especially on the off chance that you are making genuinely little exchanges, which can make it hard to be gainful over the long haul. This is likewise why markdown administrations are better for little dealers, regardless of whether fledglings or not, as the additional expenses viably have a greater effect when exchange esteems are low.

## 2. Commissions and Fees

The commissions and expenses charged by an online dealer are, to some degree clearly, something that any kind of choices broker needs to think about. It's especially significant for little dealers to utilize an intermediary with serious commission on the grounds that as we have addressed above; high commissions can be a genuine issue when making low worth exchanges. Remembering that most novices will regularly begin with genuinely low worth exchanges as well. Learners alternatives merchants additionally ought to be hoping to keep commission charges as low as could be expected under the circumstances.

You ought to likewise be searching for commission and charge structures that are quite direct. A few spots have structures that are truly tangled, and this is an additional difficulty that you just needn't bother with. You should know that various alternatives merchants will offer truly low feature commission rates, yet then have little print specifying that specific rules must be met to get the low rates. On the other hand, they may offer low commissions yet then have a heap of different expenses that get charged to your record.

## 3. Least Deposit and Minimum Trade Value

This is something different that apprentice brokers and little merchants truly need to take a gander at before joining with an online help. Most places will have fixed essentials for the amount you have to store and how much each exchange must be worth. The base sums can change essentially starting with one specialist then onto the next, and you clearly need to ensure that the figures are reasonable for you.

Plainly, on the off chance that you are making little exchanges you won't have any desire to store colossal sums at any one time so you should search for an intermediary with a generally low least store. Similarly, you will require a merchant that has genuinely low least exchange esteems to guarantee that you can make your exchanges at a level you are alright with.

The absolute most significant thing to recall while picking an online intermediary is that you ought to utilize a specialist that is appropriate to you and your prerequisites. It truly merits investing some energy doing your own exploration and looking at precisely what is on offer in light of the fact that the exact opposite thing you need to do is continually changing your merchant since things are not working out.

We emphatically propose that you accept the guidance we have offered above and furthermore adhere to those online alternatives handles that we have suggested.

# Chapter Five:
# Option Trading And Other Financial Instruments

With regards to exchanging and interest all in all, there are a wide range of money related instruments that can be utilized for potential benefits. A money related instrument is basically any tradable resource; regardless of whether it is money, proof of possession in a substance, different wares or even the authoritative option to get or convey another budgetary instrument.

Stocks are most likely the most popular budgetary instrument, yet there are additionally bonds, prospects, and obviously choices contracts. There is cash to be produced using putting resources into, or exchanging any money related instrument on the off chance that you comprehend what you are doing.

On the off chance that you are keen on alternatives exchanging, at that point you clearly need to recognize what choices contracts are and how they work. In any case, it likewise pays to have a comprehension of other budgetary instruments and how they work by method of examination. Regardless of whether your venture plan includes just exchanging alternatives, it can in any case help to discover more about other money related instruments.

You may well choose to adhere to just exchanging alternatives, yet you additionally may conclude that you need to put resources into other money related instruments as well. In this area we contrast choices with the accompanying monetary instruments:

1. Stocks

2. Bonds

3. Forex

4. Fates

5. Warrants

**Contrasts Between Stocks and Options**

If you somehow happened to ask how a great many people need to engage in contributing, at that point the most widely recognized answer would likely purchase stocks in publically recorded organizations. This is generally in light of the fact that purchasing stocks is probably the least difficult approaches to put away cash, and anybody can do it with only a tad of information.

There is unquestionably cash to be produced using purchasing or exchanging stocks and there various individuals that do precisely that. Notwithstanding, when you contrast exchanging stocks with exchanging choices, there are some unmistakable preferences that alternatives offer.

Purchasing stocks in publically recorded organizations is one of the most widely recognized ways for individuals to put away cash. When you comprehend the rudiments in question, it's generally simple to search for appropriate speculation openings that meet your venture objectives. With the wide determination of online agents, the procedure for purchasing and selling stocks is simpler than at any other time.

All things considered, numerous speculators effectively exchange stocks to make bigger returns than is conceivable through utilizing a purchase and hold technique to fabricate a portfolio which just increments in esteem after some time.

Notwithstanding, purchasing and selling stocks isn't the best way to benefit from the money related markets using any and all means and there are numerous different strategies that can be utilized. Exchanging choices is one specific type of putting that has developed essentially in prevalence: among prepared, master financial specialists however with an entire scope of individuals.

Alternatives exchanging is open to anybody and despite the fact that it's somewhat more mind boggling than simply purchasing stocks, it isn't that hard for anybody to find out about the subject and get included. One of the primary things you ought to comprehend is the manner by which putting resources into choices is not the same as putting resources into stocks, and on this page we clarify the fundamental contrasts between the two.

**Crucial Differences**

The principle distinction among stocks and choices is the way that when putting resources into stocks you are really purchasing a security that can go up or down in esteem yet when putting resources into alternatives you are purchasing a subsidiary. A subsidiary is basically an exchanging instrument that gets its incentive from some other security. The estimation of the subordinate is along these lines firmly connected to the estimation of that other security. This is known as the fundamental security, yet it can likewise be influenced by different elements.

On account of alternatives, there are different protections other than stocks; it can likewise be other money related instruments, for example, items and monetary standards. The truth of the matter is that there is an entire scope of various sorts of alternatives that can be purchased and sold methods you can estimate on a wide assortment of money related instruments when exchanging choices.

At the point when you purchase stocks in a specific organization, you are really purchasing an offer in that organization. In the event that the organization performs well, at that point the odds are that your venture will increment in worth and there are two manners by which you can make an arrival. To begin with, you can decide to sell at a greater expense than you purchased for to arrive at a higher benefit. Second, on the off chance that the organization you have put resources into is gainful, at that point they may grant investors with a yearly profit (a portion of those benefits that is paid to any individual who holds stock in the organization).

It's conceivable to make awesome returns by holding profit paying stocks for an extensive stretch of time, you despite everything own the real resource that you can decide to sell whenever. You can likewise decide to short sell stocks in an organization and cause a benefit on the off chance that they to go down in esteem.

The manner in which alternatives work is extraordinary; when you purchase investment opportunities you are really purchasing an agreement that gives you the option to purchase or sell explicit stocks at a concurred cost. While these agreements arrive in a wide range of classifications, they would all be able to be classed as either calls or puts. Calls give you the option to purchase a particular stock at a fixed value (this fixed cost is known as the strike cost) while puts give the option to sell a particular stock at a fixed cost. On the off chance that you purchase calls, the value you pay for them doesn't get you any real stock; it essentially gives you the option to get it.

So the essential distinction between these two money related instruments is very straightforward. Purchasing stocks is paying to claim a genuine offer in an organization, while purchasing alternatives is paying for the option to purchase (or sell) shares in an organization. This distinction gives exchanging choices some noteworthy points of interest.

**Favorable circumstances of Options Over Stocks**

Perhaps the greatest favorable position of purchasing brings over purchasing stock is the way that you can confine potential misfortunes while as yet profiting by potential benefits. You should put resources into a specific organization, for instance, that had a high possibility of expanding altogether in esteem yet additionally had a little danger of falling essentially in esteem. On the off chance that you purchased the stock you would profit by any ascent in esteem, however you would likewise be presented to any fall in esteem.

For instance, suppose these stocks were exchanging at $20 and you chose to purchase 1,000 offers. In the event that they went up to $30, you could sell your 1,000 offers for a benefit of $10 each. This would give you a sum of $10,000 benefit. In this way any commissions you caused for your exchanges, would simply be a special reward to your benefit. Be that as it may, in the event that they tumbled to $10 before you chose to cut your misfortunes, you would lose $10,000.

Presently assume you had chosen to purchase call alternatives on the stock rather and you purchased 1,000 calls at $1 each, giving you the option to purchase 1,000 offers at the strike cost of $20.

With the stock ascending to $30, you could then purchase the offers at $20 and promptly sell them at $30 for a benefit of $10,000. You would, obviously, need to factor in the first $1,000 you spent on the choices contracts, however you have still made a complete return of $9,000. This somewhat less than the $10,000 you would have produced using purchasing the investment opportunities, however the genuine bit of leeway here is in constraining your misfortunes.

On the off chance that the stock tumbled to $10, at that point you would just not practice your alternative, and you would just have lost the $1,000 you initially contributed. This model shows that despite the fact that you may forfeit a little level of your benefits if the value moves as arranged, you are enormously diminishing your presentation to chance if the value moves the other way.

This model likewise features another significant favorable position of alternatives over stocks, and that is influence. To claim the 1,000 offers at $20 in the above model, you would have needed to contribute $20,000. Expecting the value rose as featured for a benefit of $10,000, this would give you a half profit for your speculation.

In any case, purchasing the 1,000 choices at $1 would have implied a venture of just $1,000. With the offers ascending to $30 and an absolute benefit of $9,000 you would get a 800% profit for your speculation. Not exclusively can purchasing alternatives limit your hazard, yet it can likewise give you the potential for an a lot more prominent return comparative with your underlying venture.

This fairly fundamental model ought to furnish you with a thought of how exchanging alternatives can be a helpful method to contribute. There are various ways that exchanging choices can be utilized including supporting a current position contingent upon what systems you wish to use.

## CONTRASTS BETWEEN BONDS AND OPTION TRADING

Bonds are another extremely clear approach to contribute, and they are especially speaking to chance unfriendly financial specialists who incline toward traditionalist, safe ventures. Bonds, similar to alternatives, are a type of money related agreement between two gatherings, yet securities and choices are actually very not quite the same as one another.

At the point when a great many people consider contributing, they will in general consider purchasing stocks on the securities exchanges. Purchasing stocks is absolutely a typical type of contributing, however the monetary markets additionally offer numerous other exchanging instruments that can be purchased and offered to conceivably bring benefits back. With enough time committed to explore, finding out about the different monetary instruments that can be exchanged, and the methodologies in question, it's unquestionably workable for anybody to turn into a capable financial specialist.

Actually, with such a large number of online agents giving access to the money related markets it's simpler than any time in recent memory to engage with speculation, regardless of what starting capital is included and how much time an individual has.

In any case, numerous individuals are hesitant to do considerably more than basically put resources into stocks and offers as that typically appears the most basic and direct approach to contribute. The way that there are such huge numbers of various types of venture can appear dazing, especially to those with genuinely restricted understanding, and it regularly bodes well to simply stay with purchasing stocks. This is reasonable from various perspectives; the wide scope of budgetary instruments in the market can be befuddling.

For instance, securities and choices are both generally accessible from merchants and can both be utilized as a component of a venture system, in spite of the fact that they really have altogether different attributes. The way that they are both a type of agreement, however, can bring about individuals erroneously accepting that they are something very similar. An often posed inquiry is "What are the contrasts among alternatives and bonds?" On this page we answer that question by taking a gander at the principle contrasts and furthermore a portion of the favorable circumstances that choices exchanging has over purchasing bonds.

**Primary Differences**

Choices and bonds are both monetary agreements between two gatherings, and it's this likeness that does now and again lead to disarray. The least complex approach to feature the distinctions is to initially give a rearranged meaning of them two.

The term bond is utilized to allude to a particular sort of agreement between a borrower and a loan specialist. This agreement requires the borrower to stick to explicit terms with respect to reimbursement. The borrower is known as the backer, and they issue a declaration to the bank who turns into the holder. The authentication can be sold available, and the new holder turns into the proprietor of the obligation security.

Bonds are a sort of fixed salary security in light of the fact that the measure of intrigue payable on the credit is fixed in the agreement. Likewise, the guarantor must reimburse the first sum acquired in full when the bond lapses. Bonds are customarily given by governments and huge organizations.

An alternatives contract likewise comprises of two gatherings. The purchaser, or holder, of a choices contract has the right (however not the commitment) to purchase (a call) or sell (a put) a particular security at a fixed cost. While the holder can pick whether to practice their right, the vender, or author, of the agreement must meet their commitment whenever called upon to do as such.

Choices don't offer the holder a fixed return, and their worth can vary contingent upon value developments of the fundamental security. They can terminate useless if there is no advantage in practicing the option to purchase or sell the hidden security.

So alternatives and bonds are in reality totally different as far as the manner in which they work. Securities are fundamentally a venture vehicle for a purchase and hold methodology, given the fixed return they offer and the worth they hold dependent on the compensation out at expiry. Be that as it may, choices are exchanging instruments that can be utilized to look out at the cost developments of a wide scope of hidden protections.

Albeit both of these alternatives have a fixed lapse date, bonds offer the security of a compensation out when they terminate while choices can terminate worth nothing by any stretch of the imagination. Bonds likewise normally have extremely long lives, frequently running for a long time or more. Choices will in general have a lot shorter term contracts. The two ventures have their places in a speculation portfolio, however there are a lot more techniques for exchanging choices and there are some reasonable points of interest as well.

**Points of interest of Options Over Bonds**

Bonds are a sheltered type of speculation as they are commonly given by governments or settled organizations. This implies there is next to no danger of the holder not getting their customary returns or not getting chief entirety returned at the purpose of expiry. Notwithstanding, the profits offered by securities mirror this generally safe, and you would be probably not going to ever make generous benefits except if putting extremely noteworthy aggregates of cash into them.

Alternatives, then again, offer the potential for enormous benefits: regularly with next to no beginning capital required. They can be purchased and composed dependent on a wide assortment of hidden protections including stocks, outside monetary forms, and wares. They give an immense scope of chances for venture and hypothesis.

There are procedures for exchanging choices that can be utilized whether or not there is a buyer showcase, a bear advertise, or an impartial market. Alternatives can be exchanged under basically any condition with an opportunity of making an arrival. Most methodologies include making choices spreads which can be utilized to make solid open doors for benefit while additionally keeping the hazard to compensate proportion at a level you feel great with.

Choices exchanging is surely to some degree more perplexing than different types of contributing, however the prizes can be justified, despite all the trouble on the off chance that you are set up to invest the necessary exertion. When you comprehend the nuts and bolts of the choices market and feel good that you realize what is included, at that point beginning isn't as troublesome as you would have suspected.

**CONTRASTS BETWEEN FOREX AND OPTIONS**

Forex exchanging, exchanging outside monetary forms, has developed in ubiquity altogether as of late, and effective forex dealers can make genuine measures of cash through this method. It does, be that as it may, require a ton of time and exertion and it tends to be a distressing and extraordinary approach to contribute. Outside monetary standards are really one of the numerous budgetary instruments that can be the hidden security in choices contracts, so it's conceivable to exchange alternatives and theorize on monetary standards simultaneously.

Be that as it may, as budgetary instruments remote monetary standards and alternatives contracts are not so much comparable.

Anybody can engage with contributing generally effectively; it doesn't take as much information as individuals regularly might suspect and it's conceivable to make comes back with only a little measure of time and exertion. You don't require a tremendous measure of beginning capital. In any case, it could be viewed as a smart thought to work with a limited quantity of cash when you first begin.

What regularly makes individuals stray away from contributing is the scope of various venture vehicles that can be purchased and sold on the financial exchanges and different trades. A great many people comprehend the essential idea of purchasing and selling stocks and offers, yet when you begin considering forex exchanging, alternatives exchanging, and fates exchanging things do will in general get somewhat more entangled.

It's a great plan to see how the different money related instruments and types of exchanging vary from one another. Understanding this will help you colossally with regards to the sort of venture systems you will need to utilize and how you can accomplish your objectives. On this page we take a gander at the contrasts between exchanging forex and choices, and why we think exchanging alternatives is better.

**Basic Differences**

In numerous regards, looking at forex and choices exchanging resembles contrasting apples and oranges; they are quite various things. In any case, they are both a type of contributing and in the event that you are not totally clear on how the two things vary, at that point it can absolutely be useful to study them to maintain a strategic distance from any potential errors.

You may conclude that forex is a superior fit for your speculation objectives than alternatives, or the other way around, however without knowing precisely how they vary then it is extremely hard to make an educated judgment.

The word forex is a compound word dependent on the term outside trade, which identifies with how the estimation of various monetary standards around the globe identify with one another. The estimation of a specific money corresponding to another cash varies constantly: some of the time with extremely little developments and here and there drastically.

It's conceivable to see those variances through forex exchanging, where basically you need to attempt to anticipate how one cash will move comparative with another. This may sound unthinkable, however there are various elements included and it's conceivable to accurately anticipate forex developments through concentrated research and examination. Forex exchanging essentially includes purchasing and offering various monetary standards to exploit their value development.

Choices exchanging includes the purchasing and selling of choices contracts, which are totally different to outside monetary forms. They are as yet exchanging instruments, in that the thought is to purchase and sell at the correct time so as to make a benefit, yet they are substantially more mind boggling than remote monetary standards. A basic definition is that they are money related agreements that give the holder the option to purchase a predetermined security at a fixed cost, at or before a fixed lapse date. They can give the holder the correct sell a predetermined security at a fixed cost.

There are surely valid justifications for exchanging remote monetary forms, and there are numerous individuals who earn substantial sums of money from doing as such. Notwithstanding, when legitimately contrasting forex with choices, you will find that there are various points of interest to exchanging alternatives. We investigate these preferences beneath.

**Preferences of Options Over Forex**

Perhaps the greatest preferred position choices has over forex is the adaptability of what you can put resources into. This can prompt more prominent open doors for benefit. Forex exchanging is restricted carefully to outside monetary standards, yet you can purchase and sell choices contracts dependent on a scope of basic protections including stocks, wares, records, and prospects. Truth be told, you can exchange gets that depend on outside monetary standards as well, so you can at present guess on the forex showcase.

On the off chance that you need to be effective at exchanging forex, at that point you truly need to take part in an exceptionally itemized investigation to attempt to anticipate how the estimation of remote monetary standards will move. There are numerous variables that can impact value developments on the forex markets and in a perfect world you have to comprehend them all and the effect they can have. While research and examination has a major impact in choices exchanging as well, you don't really need to broadly expound in the event that you like to keep things straightforward.

In principle, you can keep things as straightforward as you need with regards to choices exchanging – on the off chance that you simply need to guess on specific stocks going up in esteem then you can simply purchase the fitting agreements and exercise your alternative to purchase the stock in the event that it increases in cost. In any case on the off chance that you need to get more inside and out, at that point you can get familiar with about making choices spreads that can be utilized in an assortment of techniques.

Alternatives exchanging likewise offers a specific level of hazard control which helps on the off chance that you are not happy with facing huge challenges. There are a lot of techniques you can use to constrain chance introduction; alternatives can be an extraordinary apparatus for supporting also.

**CONTRASTS BETWEEN FUTURES AND OPTIONS**

Prospects and alternatives are two money related instruments that are ordinarily utilized by financial specialists and merchants, frequently for comparative reasons. To be sure, there are numerous likenesses between the two sorts of agreements and they are every now and again mistook for one another. There is, be that as it may, one especially basic distinction between the two.

Choices and prospects are both ordinarily utilized exchanging instruments the universe of venture and account. Exchanging both of them is somewhat more convoluted than basically purchasing stocks (which is a type of venture that numerous individuals have in any event an essential comprehension of). Utilized effectively, the two of them offer a lot of chances for bringing in cash. Choices and fates are both broadly used to profit by influence and they are additionally both valuable devices for supporting purposes.

Anyway choices and prospects are in reality altogether different from one another. Regardless of this reality, they are frequently mistaken for one another and financial specialists that don't completely see how they vary from one another can tragically think choices exchanging is basically a similar thing as prospects exchanging.

This can be an exorbitant misstep, and nobody ought to ever engage with any sort of money related exchanging or speculation without knowing precisely what they are doing. On this page we feature the similitudes among choices and fates, take a gander at the principle distinction between the two, and clarify why we accept choices exchanging offers numerous points of interest.

**Similitudes Between The Two**

It ought to be clarified that there are sure similitudes among choices and fates, and it is reasonable how even generally experienced financial specialists can get the two confounded. They are both money related agreements that exist between two gatherings – the purchaser and merchant of a basic resource. The two of them can be exchanged on open trades, albeit a portion of the more perplexing agreements are just sold over the counter.

They are likewise both utilized subordinates – despite the fact that on the off chance that you comprehend what this implies the odds are that you would already be able to perceive the contrast between the two. Essentially, a subordinate is a money related instrument that gets its worth basically from at least one basic resource. Influence is a term for any procedure that you use to adequately increase the intensity of your capital.

For instance, on the off chance that you purchase stocks in an organization, at that point you truly own an offer in that organization and the advantage you own can go up or down in esteem. When purchasing a subordinate, you are purchasing an agreement which is esteemed by the hidden resource on which it's based and conceivably different factors, for example, the length of the agreement.

Influence is the point at which you successfully increase the intensity of the money you are contributing to create bigger returns; this is conceivable with the two alternatives and fates and is the fundamental motivation behind why they are known as influence subsidiaries.

**Significant Differences Between Futures And Option Trading**

The essential contrast among alternatives and prospects is in the commitments of the gatherings in question. The holder of a choices contract has the option to purchase the basic resource at a fixed cost, however not the commitment. The essayist, or dealer, of the agreement is committed to sell the holder the hidden security (or get it), if the holder chooses to practice their choice.

This clearly puts the holder of an agreement at a favorable position, in such a case that the hidden security moves against them, they can just allow the agreement to lapse and not acquire any misfortunes far beyond the first expense. On the off chance that the fundamental security moves the correct way for the holder (and in this way against the author), at that point the essayist must respect their commitment.

In a fates contract, the two gatherings are obliged to satisfy the provisions of the agreement at the purpose of lapse. This is an exceptionally noteworthy contrast. Purchasing a prospects contract where you will be obliged to purchase a specific security at a fixed value conveys considerably more hazard than purchasing an alternatives contract where you reserve the privilege to purchase a specific security at a fixed cost, yet are not obliged to proceed with it if that security neglects to climb in an incentive as you anticipate. The two gatherings associated with a fates contract are viably presented to boundless obligation.

The costs included are likewise extraordinary. At the point when an alternatives contract is first composed, its essayist offers it to the purchaser and gets the cash that the purchaser pays. Contingent upon the provisions of the agreement, the basic security included, and the conditions of the essayist, the author may must have a specific measure of edge close by. They may likewise be required to top up that edge if the basic security moves against them. Nonetheless, the purchaser possesses those agreements out and out and no further supports will be required from them.

With prospects, however, as the two gatherings are presented to misfortunes contingent upon what direction the cost of the hidden security moves, they are both required to have a specific measure of edge close by. Value contrasts on fates are settled day by day, and either gathering could be dependent upon an edge call if the estimation of the fundamental security has moved against them. This contributes to a great extent to why fates exchanging is commonly viewed as more dangerous than choices exchanging. Beneath we take a gander at several the points of interest exchanging alternatives brings to the table.

**Points of interest of Options Over Futures**

As referenced above, when exchanging fates you are conceivably presented to large misfortunes whichever side of the agreement you are on. In the event that you have the commitment to purchase a hidden security at a fixed cost and the security moves fundamentally over that fixed value, at that point you could lose generous totals. On the other hand, on the off chance that you have the commitment to sell a fundamental security at a fixed cost and the security moves altogether beneath that fixed value then you could encounter sizable misfortunes.

On the off chance that you are composing alternatives agreements and assuming a commitment to either purchase or sell a hidden security at a fixed value, at that point you are presented to comparable dangers. Be that as it may, you can exchange choices simply by purchasing contracts and not keeping in touch with them. This implies you can constrain your potential misfortunes on every single exchange you make to the measure of cash you put resources into purchasing explicit agreements.

At whatever point you purchase choices gets, the most dire outcome imaginable is that they terminate useless and you lose your underlying speculation. Regardless of whether you would like to compose contracts notwithstanding getting them, you can undoubtedly make spreads to guarantee that your misfortunes are constantly constrained. The potential for restricted liabilities in choices exchanging is a significant preferred position, especially for those that are against high hazard ventures.

Another huge favorable position alternatives exchanging offers is adaptability. There are various systems that you can use to make spreads that empower you to benefit from multi-directional value developments. For instance, you could make a spread that would bring about benefit if the basic security went down in esteem a smidgen, or on the off chance that it remained stable, or on the off chance that it went up in an incentive by any sum. This would possibly bring about restricted misfortunes if the fundamental security went down a critical sum.

With prospects contracts, you can commonly just bring in cash from the basic security moving the correct way for you. There could be boundless misfortunes if your speculation moves off course or if an unbiased outcome happens.

**CONTRASTS BETWEEN WARRANTS AND OPTIONS**

Bunches of budgetary instruments are totally not the same as one another, while many are actually very comparable. Warrants and choices are two monetary instruments that are similar in numerous regards which regularly prompts financial specialists and merchants accepting they are about something very similar. While they do share numerous qualities, there are two or three critical contrasts between the two which are imperative to perceive.

Choices contracts are on a very basic level not quite the same as most other monetary instruments, but then numerous individuals do in any case get choices exchanging mistook for different types of exchanging, for example, forex exchanging or stock exchanging. It's a word of wisdom for anybody that has any enthusiasm for exchanging or contributing to truly comprehend the different money related instruments that can be purchased and sold and how they vary from one another.

Of all the money related instruments that can be exchanged on trades and markets the world over, it's really warrants that are the most like alternatives. On this page we give data on how warrants work, and how they are unique in relation to alternatives. We likewise take a gander at a portion of the points of interest that we accept choices offer.

**Significant Differences Between The Two**

Warrants and choices are fundamentally the same as and they are frequently viewed as basically something very similar yet just with an alternate name simply like stocks and offers are essentially the equivalent. In any case, there are contrasts between the two and it's significant that you perceive these distinctions and what they mean for the financial specialist. Despite the fact that they share a great deal of similar qualities, there two or three key parts of warrants that make them very particular from choices.

The meaning of an alternatives agreement can be streamlined as follows: a monetary agreement that concedes the holder the right, yet not the commitment, to either purchase or sell a basic security at a concurred cost by a lapse date. These agreements can be named either calls, which give the holder the option to purchase the basic security, or puts which give the holder the option to sell the fundamental security.

They can likewise be either American style where the holder can practice their entitlement to purchase or sell the hidden security whenever up to and including the termination date, or European style which must be practiced on the lapse date.

In their run of the mill structure, warrants are fundamentally the same as European style call choices, in that they give the holder the option to purchase a hidden security at a fixed cost on a fixed lapse date. Be that as it may, alternatives contracts are ordinarily composed by either private speculators or market creators, and the fundamental security can be a wide assortment of money related instruments. Warrants, in any case, are composed by organizations with the hidden security being stock in the giving organization.

For instance, Company X would compose warrants dependent on the basic security of a Company X stock. Warrants can be American style as well, yet call warrants of an European style are the most well-known. In the event that the holder of a warrant needs to sell it, it is sold back to the giving organization instead of to another broker or financial specialist.

So in spite of the fact that the essential rule of the two money related instruments is fundamentally the same as, there is a huge contrast as far as who is composing the agreement. While most alternatives follow a specific normalized system, warrants are basically redone accurately to suit the giving organization and what they are attempting to accomplish.

For instance, while the length of choices are estimated in months, warrants can be, and regularly are, estimated in years and will in general have an any longer life expectancy. Due to the way that they are exceptionally tweaked, warrants are commonly exchanged over the counter markets as opposed to the publically exchanged trades.

Warrants are given by organizations for an assortment of reasons; they are regularly connected to bonds so as to make the bonds an increasingly alluring choice for speculators. They can likewise be joined to favored stock and can even be utilized in private value bargains. One of the other fundamental contrasts is that practiced alternatives dependent on stock include the deal and acquisition of existing stock, while practiced call warrants bring about the organization giving new portions of stock.

## Points of interest of Options Over Warrants

Regardless of the likenesses between the two instruments, the distinctions that exist loan certain points of interest to utilizing alternatives in an exchanging system as opposed to warrants. Perhaps the most compelling motivation to exchange alternatives is the capacity to make spreads, which can be utilized for various purposes. These spreads can be made in various manners, yet they normally include all the while purchasing and composing alternatives contracts.

While warrants can in any case speak to a strong interest in their own right, there are fundamentally less exchanging methodologies that can be utilized including warrants than those including alternatives. Likewise, as they are commonly exchanged over the counter, they are not as simple to purchase and sell as choices contracts. They are to a great extent exchanged on the trades and in this way significantly more available.

Since warrants are composed distinctly by organizations whose own stock is the fundamental security, or by a monetary establishment speaking to that organization, it's impractical to take a short situation on them and bring in cash from the stock going down in esteem. This decreases the quantity of potential open doors for making benefit contrasted with alternatives which can be utilized to benefit from stock and other monetary instruments going down in an incentive just as up.

In rundown, purchasing warrants can unquestionably be a smart thought in the correct conditions yet choices offer more prominent openness and flexibility to brokers.

## LEVELS OF TRADING AT OPTION BROKERS

When you have chosen a suitable alternatives merchant for your prerequisites, you at that point will commonly need to experience a genuinely long endorsement process before your record will be opened and prepared to utilize. You need to experience this procedure with the goal that your representative can do a hazard evaluation and choose what exchanging level, or endorsement level, you ought to be allocated.

Exchanging choices isn't as straightforward as simply joining with an intermediary and afterward making whatever exchanges you need; the dangers associated with specific exchanges and techniques implies that dealers must be dependable and just permit people to make exchanges that are appropriate for them. For instance, a total tenderfoot with a limited quantity of beginning capital wouldn't be permitted to begin utilizing complex techniques with boundless hazard presentation.

Exchanging levels are basically how representatives control the degree of hazard that their clients, and themselves, are presented to. On this page we clarify these levels in more detail, covering the accompanying:

1. The Purpose of Trading Levels

2. How Trading Levels are Assigned

3. What Each Trading Level Allows

4. Expanding your Trading Level

**1. The Purpose of Trading Levels**

The motivation behind exchanging levels, otherwise called endorsement levels, is basically to give a type of security to both the dealer and the client. Alternatives representatives are managed and have an obligation to pay special mind to the eventual benefits of their clients, which gives them a type of commitment to guarantee that their clients just face challenges in which they have adequate experience and assets for.

It isn't completely extraordinary for financial specialists and brokers to utilize high hazard procedures when they don't generally have the foggiest idea what they are doing and don't have the essential capital. In the event that things turn out badly the intermediary is possibly at risk, so they evaluate their clients and appoint them exchanging levels so they can just ever do exchanges which are similar with their experience and their financing. By doing this, both the client and the dealer are shielded from over the top introduction to hazard.

## 2. How Trading Levels are Assigned

At the point when you join with a choices intermediary, you will as a rule need to give nitty gritty data about your funds and past speculations that you have made. You will ordinarily be posed a progression of inquiries that will enable the dealer to comprehend your degree of information and hazard resilience.

Your application will at that point be checked on by the consistence division and they will figure out what exchanging level you ought to be doled out dependent on the data you have given. Now and again, you might be required to give confirmation of specific parts of your application.

Basically, intermediaries worry about two principle factors when appointing you your underlying exchanging level: your applicable experience and your general budgetary position. Experienced financial specialists that can show they have a strong information on alternatives exchanging will for the most part be appointed a more significant level in light of the fact that there is a suspicion that they realize what they are doing.

Those with a high total assets or a lot of beginning capital will likewise will in general be given a high exchanging level as well.

## 3. What Each Trading Level Allows

Most alternatives representatives appoint exchanging levels from 1 to 5; with 1 being the least and 5 being the most noteworthy. A dealer with a low exchanging level will be genuinely constrained in the procedures they can utilize, while one with the most noteworthy will have the option to make practically whatever exchange they need.

Similarly that facilitates all have their own techniques for allotting exchanging levels, they additionally for the most part have somewhat various methods of grouping exchanging methodologies. Along these lines, there is anything but an authoritative rundown of what systems each exchanging level permits at each agent; this is something that you should discover straightforwardly from your choices merchant. We can, in any case, give an unpleasant thought of what you can normally do at each level.

With an exchanging level of 1, you'll likely just have the option to purchase and compose choices where you have a comparing position in the basic security. For instance, in the event that you claimed stock in Company X, at that point you would have the option to submit a purchase to open request for put alternatives on Company X stock. This would give you the option to sell your stock at a concurred strike cost and the main extra hazard you would be presented to is the measure of cash it expenses to utilize those choices.

You would likewise have the option to put in an offer to open request accessible if the need arises alternatives on Company X stock, giving another person the option to purchase your stock at a concurred cost. Despite the fact that you would in fact make a misfortune if Company X stock went up in cost and you had to sell it underneath showcase esteem; there's no extra presentation hazard since you effectively own the stock.

An exchanging level of 2 would regularly permit you to likewise purchase call choices and put choices without having a comparing position in the basic security. You would possibly have the option to purchase alternatives contracts on the off chance that you had the assets to do so which implies there is certifiably not an enormous measure of hazard included. The most dire outcome imaginable is that the agreements terminate useless and you lose the assets contributed, yet you were unable to lose anything else than your underlying buy. This exchanging level is normally the most reduced one doled out.

Exchanging level 3 would for the most part permit the composition of alternatives for the motivations behind making charge spreads. Charge spreads are choices spreads that require a forthright expense and your misfortunes are typically restricted to that forthright cost. In spite of the fact that charge spreads include composing choices without a comparing position in the basic security, the misfortunes are constrained by having various situations on alternatives contracts dependent on that equivalent hidden security.

For instance, you could make a charge spread by composing call alternatives on a specific stock and purchasing call choices on a similar stock. Once more, there's not a gigantic measure of hazard related with these exchanges, yet the higher exchanging level is required because of the extra complexities of making spreads.

For the making of credit spreads, where you get a forthright credit and are presented to future misfortunes if the spread doesn't proceed as arranged, you would regularly require a record with exchanging level 4. This is on the grounds that potential misfortunes are progressively hard to compute. Exchanging level 5, being the most noteworthy, would fundamentally give you the opportunity to make whatever exchanges you needed. You would, notwithstanding, for the most part be required to have a lot of alternatives edge in your record.

**4. Expanding your Trading Level**

There's no particular method to ensure an expanded exchanging level with your representative. A few representatives may survey your record occasionally and naturally increment it if suitable, yet this is very uncommon. You would as a rule need to contact your dealer legitimately and demand an overhaul, yet this would be totally at the tact of your financier firm. On the off chance that you had a strong exchanging history with them and a sensible measure of assets on account, at that point you would presumably have a decent potential for success of being redesigned.

To get the most advantage out this guide you should peruse all the articles in the endorsed request. The greater part of what is incorporated is generally direct, in spite of the fact that there are a couple of progressively complex subjects included as well. Perusing it all together should assist you with ensuring that everything bodes well and know nothing is actually too hard to even think about understanding.

# Chapter Six:
# Beginning Formal Preparation

This article covers the initial steps you should take to guarantee that you are prepared to start exchanging choices. We talk about the information base that you need and the significance of plainly characterizing what it is you need to accomplish. We additionally give subtleties on the best way to get ready to an exchanging plan and why an exchanging plan is a basic apparatus in choices exchanging.

The initial step you should take before risking your cash is to ensure that you know all that you have to think about alternatives exchanging. This doesn't imply that you need to know totally everything that there is to think about alternatives and how they are exchanged, yet as a base you ought to be comfortable with what is included, how choices work, the various sorts of agreements, and the various kinds of requests.

You ought to likewise have in any event an essential comprehension of how spreads are made on the grounds that, they are the essential segments of all alternatives exchanging procedures. You'll additionally need to know about the most significant wording that is utilized.

When you have the fundamental information base, you are prepared to proceed onward to the following stage and should begin considering your very own conditions and how they will influence what you will be doing. You ought to particularly be pondering how much time you will spend on your exchanging: not simply as far as really putting in your requests, yet additionally as far as doing your exploration and investigation and arranging your individual exchanges.

You ought to likewise turn out to be the manner by which you are going to do your exploration and examination. You will likewise need to choose how much cash you will contribute; with your beginning capital, you should choose whether or not you will include that beginning capital as you come. These are the kind of contemplations that will assist you with putting your exchanging plan, which we will discuss later.

**Characterizing Your Objectives**

The following piece of your readiness is one of the most significant things you have to do before beginning; characterizing your goals. There is no point engaging in alternatives exchanging except if you have an away from of precisely what it is you are planning to accomplish. It's fairly deceitful for your target to just be "to bring in cash" – you truly should be more exact than that.

In the event that you are beginning on low maintenance premise while holding down an occupation, at that point your first objective might be bring in enough cash so you can find employment elsewhere and exchange full time. On the off chance that that is one of your targets, at that point you should know how much cash you should make for that to be a reality and how much cash you have to have saved for crises. On the off chance that you are going straight into exchanging full time, at that point you ought to have an objective for how much cash you need to make on a month to month premise.

Regardless of whether you are hoping to enhance your current salary or supplant it doesn't generally make a difference. Your goal could even be to put a smidgen of additional cash aside every month to help subsidize your retirement or your youngsters' training. The concentration here is to ensure that you do have targets set up. In the event that you comprehend what your objectives are, at that point it turns out to be a lot simpler to assemble an arrangement that can assist you with accomplishing them. You additionally have something to quantify your prosperity against.

In the event that you don't have a clue what it is you are attempting to accomplish, at that point it's difficult to know whether you are in good shape. Preferably you ought to have momentary objectives and long haul objectives, and they can generally be adaptable if your conditions change. You simply should be certain that you generally have something to take a stab at on the grounds that, this will likewise assist you with keeping yourself propelled above whatever else.

**Composing a Trading Plan**

When you have followed the above advances, the following phase of your arrangement is to compose your exchanging plan. This is an imperative piece of the foundation you ought to do before you start, and this is something you should put a lot of ime and exertion into. While characterizing your destinations gives you something to focus on, it is your arrangement that spreads out how you are going to acheive those targets.

With a reasonable exchanging plan you are fundamentally setting yourself your own rules for how you will move toward things and giving the parameters to what you will do, when you will do it, and how you will do it.

There are various focuses that you ought to know about with regards to composing an exchanging plan. To begin with, there aren't generally any rights and wrongs, other than the way that it's correct that you set up an arrangement. Your arrangement will be close to home to you, and it ought to mirror your own conditions, your own goal, and the best methods for you to accomplish your targets.

Also, you truly can't and ought not belittle exactly that it is so critical to compose an exchanging plan. Such huge numbers of financial specialists and merchants don't waste time with an arrangement and simply jump into things with no reasonable heading, which perpetually doesn't end up being admirably. A decent arrangement can assist you with keeping away from a great deal of the slip-ups that novices make, and help you in keeping up a solid spotlight on what you ought to do and when.

It ought to likewise be noticed that any arrangement you compose can be balanced later on. While it is essential to follow any arrangement that you have set up, it can change after some time. For instance your conditions may change, maybe implying that you have less time to spend on your exchanging, as it's just right that you ought to correct your arrangement in like manner.

Likewise, as you acquire experience you may choose to begin utilizing an alternate methodology, you may decide to utilize further developed methodologies. Once more, you should make the important changes to mirror your new methodology.

In all actuality, your exchanging plan ought to be under consistent survey and you shouldn't be stressed over making any modifications that might be required. You simply need to ensure that you do adhere to doing whatever the arrangement you have set up recommends you do.

In spite of the fact that, as we have referenced, there are no particular rights and wrongs to composing your exchanging plan, there is a sure structure that you ought to follow regarding the components that ought to be incorporated. Underneath, we have recorded the significant components that you should include.

**Exchanging Objectives:** This is presumably the absolute most significant piece of your exchanging plan. There are various purposes behind having unmistakably characterized goals, a large portion of which we have just referenced previously. Goals give you something substantial to focus on, and they assist you with keeping centered and remain inspired. You ought to incorporate any transient objectives you have set yourself, notwithstanding your more drawn out term desire. You should likewise fuse some type of course of events for when you intend to hit your principle targets.

**Overseeing Time:** Good time the executives is a major piece of fruitful alternatives exchanging. In spite of the fact that it might take just a couple of seconds to really make an exchange, there is much more required than simply the putting in of requests. Anyway much time you have accessible for your exchanging, you should ensure that you distribute sufficient opportunity to do all that you have to do: including doing examination and investigation, and arranging your exchanges. In a perfect world, your arrangement ought to specify precisely what you will be doing and when.

Inquiring about Potential Trades: To give yourself the most obvious opportunity with regards to using sound judgment, you should do a decent measure of research to attempt to feature appropriate open doors for potential exchanges. Your arrangement ought to incorporate what kind of strategies you will use to complete this exploration.

**Overseeing Risk and Capital:** You ought to have an away from of what level of hazard you are OK with taking and how much beginning capital you need to contribute; this ought to be reflected in your arrangement. You ought to likewise clarify precisely how you will deal with your hazard introduction and how you will deal with your spending plan.

Choosing Trades: Somewhat clearly, a key piece of choices exchanging is choosing what exchanges to make and when to make them. Your arrangement should spread out your procedure for doing this.

**Surveying Performance:** Assessing your own presentation is another significant part of exchanging alternatives, yet it's something dreadfully numerous individuals would prefer not to manage. By observing your exchanges and monitoring your outcomes, it's a lot simpler to see where you are committing errors and where you are hitting the nail on the head. Consequently, this will assist you with improving your aptitudes which ought to eventually assist you with getting more cash.

On the off chance that you can assemble a definite arrangement that incorporates these components, you'll as of now be in a far more grounded position than a great deal of brokers who don't invest the necessary energy and exertion to be appropriately arranged. While it is in no way, shape or form an assurance of colossal benefits, it will absolutely give you a greatly improved possibility of being fruitful and meeting your targets.

On the off chance that you are uncertain about how to move toward a portion of the things recorded above, kindly continue perusing this manual for beginning, as we offer exhortation on some of these subjects later on in this area.

**Reproduced Options Trading**

On the off chance that you need to begin choices exchanging feeling completely arranged and with a great deal of certainty, at that point you might need to think about a time of reenacted exchanging, or paper exchanging. This would fundamentally include investing a time of energy following your exchanging plan, however just creation hypothetical exchanges – for example you do everything precisely as your arrangement specifies yet rather than really making the exchanges, you simply track what exchanges you have made and at what cost.

By doing this, you can perceive how your arrangement works out for you before putting away any cash. This allows you to calibrate your arrangement and the procedures you are utilizing, if essential, and the certainty to realize that you are doing the correct things at the ideal time.

You can paper exchanges basically by keeping precise records of the hypothetical exchanges you are making. Nonetheless, you will locate that a great deal of the best online intermediaries have mimicked exchanging stages that permit you to make theoretical exchanges a similar way that you would make exchanges the typical way. They will even save your records for you, so you can without much of a stretch get a thought of how you would proceed as long as you were following your exchanging plan.

**PICKING A BROKER**

The simplest method to purchase and sell choices is through an online merchant. Our article on picking an online merchant covers all the various variables that you ought to consider when you are choosing which of the numerous accessible specialists you wish to join with. These incorporate the commission rate and the nature of the exchanging stage. Picking the correct specialist truly is a critical choice and one that you should invest some time and energy into.

Of the considerable number of choices you make preceding really beginning to exchange choices, the decision of which online alternatives merchant to utilize is in actuality one of the more significant ones. Obviously, such a choice isn't irreversible on the grounds that, you can generally utilize an alternate representative if the first you attempt doesn't exactly work out for you. Be that as it may, it merits investing energy choosing which one to join with before all else.

Utilizing the correct dealer truly can positively affect your exchanging. Online intermediaries are continually improving and they for the most part make the entire procedure for purchasing and selling alternatives significantly more proficient and simple to do. That is just evident, however, in the event that you utilize one of the top merchants that are truly adept at giving a five star administration.

The procedure for picking a dealer isn't actually hard, yet there is a great deal to consider. There are such huge numbers of decisions out there and despite the fact that they all in fact offer a similar sort of administration, some of them may be more reasonable for you than others. Few out of every odd merchant will have the very same prerequisites which makes it hard to absolutely say that a particular intermediary is "the best." What may be directly for one dealer may not really be directly for another.

The key is truly to work out what is critical to you and afterward do some exploration to discover which intermediary is probably going to be the most helpful for your very own needs.

We have secured a portion of the fundamental factors that you ought to consider:

1. Commissions and Fees

2. Speed and Quality of Order Execution

3. Exchanging Platform and Ease of Use

4. Safety efforts

5. Notoriety

6. Client assistance

7. Extra Considerations

**1. Commissions and Fees**

It's fairly legitimate that one of the most significant contemplations while picking an online merchant is the thing that the charges are. Charges can fundamentally be separated into two primary classifications: commissions and different expenses.

Commissions are charged on each exchange that you make, regardless of whether you are purchasing or selling alternatives, thus it can clearly signify a sizable aggregate on the off chance that you are making a great deal of exchanges. A few intermediaries likewise have a base commission and this is something to pay special mind to on the off chance that you are wanting to make various little exchanges; some may charge higher commissions relying upon what kind of choice is being executed.

The extra expenses can incorporate an entire scope of various charges including a yearly charge just for having a record, charges for stores and withdrawals, or additional expenses for making specific kinds of requests.

Contingent upon what procedures and exchanging styles you are utilizing, you might be making exchanges that will just create benefits that are moderately little contrasted with the sum contributed. It isn't at all phenomenal for alternatives brokers to work on very close edges, and this makes it imperative to decrease the costs associated with making exchanges.

Regardless of whether you will in general make exchanges that have higher edges, there is as yet a conspicuous advantage to diminishing expenses because,quite just, lower costs mean more benefit. Perhaps the greatest cost engaged with exchanging choices is, similarly as with any monetary instrument, obviously the commissions and expenses that are brought about when making exchanges.

In this manner, before you join at a representative you ought to know about their bonus structure and any extra expenses that can be applied so you can be totally certain that their charges are appropriate for the manner in which you will exchange. Nonetheless, it's likewise significant that commissions and expenses aren't really its finish. They are unmistakably significant, however somewhat the facts confirm that you get what you pay for. The least expensive intermediaries are not really the best, and it tends to merit paying somewhat more on the off chance that you feel an increasingly costly representative is better for you in different territories.

One specific purpose behind paying more would be in the event that you needed some assistance while you were beginning. Most online specialists are known as rebate intermediaries since they keep their payments low and their administration is fundamentally just to execute the requests that you teach them to. There are additionally full assistance intermediaries, which regularly charge at a higher rate, however give you the advantage of an accomplished proficient close by to offer you counsel and direction.

Such help can wind up being important, so a full assistance dealer might merit considering; you can generally change to a rebate intermediary once you gain the experience and certainty to go only it.

## 2. Speed and Quality of Order Execution

The speed of which an online representative can execute your requests is another key factor that ought to be considered. On the off chance that your merchant doesn't complete your exchanges in a convenient manner, it can negatively affect how your request is filled and may even bring about your request not getting filled by any stretch of the imagination. The best ones will ordinarily execute your requests as fast as could be expected under the circumstances and will have the option to guarantee you that they are executed at the most ideal cost. Getting the most flawlessly awesome costs accessible can have a major effect to your primary concern, so this truly is something you need progressed admirably.

On a comparative note, you additionally might need to utilize an online representative that has a quick and responsive webpage as the choices market can move rapidly to be sure. In the event that your merchant's site is refreshing too gradually, or you are encountering a postpone when attempting to move between one page and another, at that point this can possibly prompt diminished benefits, botched chances, or even critical misfortunes on the off chance that you are attempting to put in a request.

In spite of the fact that not explicitly identified with picking an intermediary, this is a fitting time to specify the significance of having exceptional innovation. You ought to have not too bad present day gear and a dependable web association on the off chance that you will be exchanging choices on the web.

## 3. Exchanging Platform and Ease of Use

Choices exchanging is perplexing enough as of now without the additional inconveniences of utilizing an online specialist that has an exchanging stage which is difficult to utilize. The exact opposite thing you need to do is need to invest any additional energy making sense of how to discover the data you are searching for or experiencing a laborious procedure for putting in your requests. You truly need to utilize an intermediary that has an easy to use interface, a basic requesting system, and different highlights that help with generally usefulness.

## 4. Safety efforts

In the event that you have a record with an online agent and you have your own cash stopped with them, you need to be certain that your record is secure and not at risk to be hacked. Sadly, that is an advanced hazard that accompanies utilizing on the web innovation to make money related exchanges. The top online specialists utilize the most recent safety efforts to guarantee that they are totally shielded from outside obstruction and that your record and any private subtleties that you give stay safe consistently.

## 5. Notoriety

The best online specialists will by and large have gained notoriety for themselves and have solid track records of offering great assistance to their clients. On the off chance that you stick to utilizing those that have great notorieties, at that point the odds are exceptionally high that you will have a positive encounter.

Before you open a record with anybody, you should seriously mull over doing a web search and checking whether there is negative criticism about them anyplace on the web. On the other hand, you should ensure that you just sign up with an organization that comes suggested by a respectable source, for example, the online dealers that we list on this website. We are specific about the proposals we make to our perusers and just rundown those that have a solid notoriety.

## 6. Client care

In spite of the fact that you would trust that everything goes easily consistently, the odds are that you will experience some specialized challenges or issues or some likeness thereof at some point. This is the reason the degree of client assistance offered by an agent is additionally a consider worth considering. On the off chance that you are utilizing an OK one, at that point any issues will most likely be rare, however they will in any case happen once in a while and it's ideal to realize that there is OK client assistance accessible to give you some help when you need it.

## 7. Extra Considerations

The previously mentioned factors are likely the most significant, yet there are some extra contemplations that are likewise worth considering. For instance, your exchanging plan may be founded completely on exchanging alternatives however there might be the odd event when you need to expand and put resources into other money related instruments. On the off chance that you think this is plausible, at that point you should be taking a gander at representatives that are likewise appropriate for purchasing and selling other budgetary instruments.

You may likewise need to consider what choices are accessible in the event that you can't make your exchanges on the web. On the off chance that you have to make an exchange yet don't approach the web, at that point you would need an elective method of putting orders. On the off chance that this is something that you think could be an issue for you then you ought to consider representatives that offer different approaches to make exchanges and convey.

There are likewise a few monetary related contemplations. Something that may be especially applicable for fledgling brokers is the base measure of store required. Various online specialists have high least store sums, and in the event that you are anticipating beginning with a generally low beginning capital, at that point this could be an issue for you. You should look at what the base store is before joining anyplace, and guarantee that it's an appropriate sum for your own financial plan.

The other monetary related thought is the thing that impetuses may be accessible. Since there are such a large number of online agents around, the commercial center has gotten extremely serious and intermediaries are continually trying new advantages to draw in more clients. One way they do this is by offering merchants motivators for joining with them.

Such motivating forces can incorporate decreased or free commissions for a while or some free assets added to your first store. A tad of free cash isn't sufficient explanation without anyone else to pick a specific dealer except if they likewise meet a large portion of your different prerequisites, yet on the off chance that you are attempting to pick between two intermediaries, at that point going with the one with the best sign up offer is certifiably not an awful method to choose. Know, however, that these motivators as a rule accompany certain terms and conditions so you should ensure you recognize what duties you need to make.

The last factor that you may need to consider is the exchanging levels that are accessible to you. Regardless of whether this is pertinent to you to a great extent relies upon precisely how you plan on utilizing alternatives contracts. In the event that you just arrangement on utilizing alternatives as a feature of a supporting procedure, to secure a current portfolio, at that point exchanging levels won't generally be applicable to you.

Basically every online intermediary will permit you to compose call alternatives or purchase put choices on basic protections that you effectively own in light of the fact that, you aren't generally facing any extra challenge, yet simply supporting against your protections falling in esteem. Nonetheless, in the event that you plan on utilizing choices theoretically without possessing the pertinent basic security, at that point exchanging levels will be an issue for you.

In the event that you just arrangement on purchasing alternatives with the end goal of practicing or selling them for a benefit, at that point most merchants will likewise permit you to do that, giving you have the assets to do as such. In the event that you are utilizing methodologies that include composing alternatives and in this way choices edge, at that point exchanging levels are something you have to consider.

At the point when you join with an alternatives merchant, they will do a hazard appraisal to figure out what level of hazard is reasonable for you, and your record will at that point be allocated a specific exchanging level. This will basically specify the fitting degree of choices edge and somewhat will impact what methodologies you can utilize. In this manner, on the off chance that you are anticipating utilizing a portion of the more perplexing procedures that require choices edge, you have to take a gander at what the prerequisites are of an online agent for being relegated the exchanging level that you need.

# Chapter Seven:
# Recognizing Trading Opportunities

A key piece of alternatives exchanging is centers around discovering chances to make exchanges. There are various ways that you can recognize and survey such chances, and we have given data on what is engaged with the procedure. To be effective in your exchanging, you will have a lot of chances for exchanges, so this is unquestionably something you should submit some an opportunity to.

On the off chance that you have been perusing this guide so as to assist you with beginning with alternatives exchanging, you will thoroughly understand the underlying readiness required and how to pick a merchant. You''ll additionally have a comprehension of exchanging levels and how they can influence your capacity to utilize certain procedures.

At this stage it's an ideal opportunity to begin pondering how you are going to discover chances to exchange. You could know totally everything there is to think about choices exchanging, however such information is just valuable in the event that you can really try everything and recognize chances to make a few benefits.

Despite the fact that alternatives exchanging is actually very perplexing, anybody that is set up to invest energy learning the subject can eventually be effective. Be that as it may, realizing how to exchange alternatives isn't sufficient without anyone else; you have to realize how to bring in cash out of it. This takes difficult work and responsibility since, you should invest the necessary exertion so as to locate the correct chances and afterward make the proper exchanges.

In the event that you can do that reliably, at that point you will very likely accomplish your objectives. On this page we take a gander at how you approach distinguishing possibly beneficial open doors for exchanging choices.

1. Which Underlying Assets?

2. Doing Research

3. Central and Technical Analysis

**1. Which Underlying Assets?**

Despite the fact that choices contracts are resources themselves, they are really subordinates that get their incentive from the hidden resources which they identify with. Choices agreements can be purchased and sold on a wide scope of basic resources that incorporate stocks, remote monetary forms, wares, and lists.

This makes choices exchanging a truly adaptable type of contributing in light of the fact that, you can make speculations on a wide range of monetary instruments just by purchasing and selling choices contracts. This implies one of the principal things you have to consider whenever you are searching for potential choices exchanging openings is actually which of these money related instruments you need to incorporate.

We ought to be evident that you don't have to choose to exchange just investment opportunities, or just forex choices, or just file alternatives. You can purchase and sell the same number of various sorts of choices as you feel great with. Be that as it may, you do need to consider how you will be examining potential exchanges and how you'll be recognizing appropriate chances.

On the off chance that you concluded that you would think about a wide range of various hidden protections, at that point you would be giving yourself the most obvious opportunity with regards to discovering openings due to the wide scope of conceivable outcomes. You would should be readied, however, to complete a great deal of investigation into various money related markets which could be very tedious and it could really make it exceptionally hard to locate the quantity of chances as you might want.

On the other hand, on the off chance that you concluded that you were just going to exchange investment opportunities dependent on stocks in a specific division, at that point you would have the option to concentrate your examination explicitly on publically recorded organizations that work around there. You may wind up turning into a specialist in that field and be significantly more adroit at distinguishing related open doors dependent on this skill.

The drawback, obviously, to adopting such a restricted strategy is, that you might be passing up loads of different open doors in various segments and markets that you aren't in any event, taking a gander at.

There truly is no correct way, or incorrect way, to move toward this part of distinguishing openings and we wouldn't offer a particular guidance in such manner. All we would recommend is that you set aside the effort to consider which fundamental resources you need to incorporate and afterward it's eventually down to what you feel great with and what you think will give you the most obvious opportunity with regards to progress.

On the off chance that you do have solid information about a specific segment or market, at that point it would bode well to use that information, however there is likewise nothing amiss with taking a more extensive view either. You may conclude that you would prefer not to inquire about and investigate the fundamental resources of alternatives, yet would prefer to contemplate the value developments of the choices contracts themselves and exchange in like manner.

## 2. Doing Research

The coming of the plan and online innovation has influenced exchanging and interest in more than one way. Not just has it brought about online dealers, which make the entire procedure of purchasing and selling of monetary instruments a lot simpler, it has additionally made data identifying with money related instruments significantly more open.

The web gives a for all intents and purposes boundless flexibly of data that can be utilized for look into purposes, and this truly is significant to financial specialists. It's fundamental to begin checking the trades to get modern statements and to follow universal news that can influence the business sectors. In any event, getting money related reports on publically recorded organizations is something essential to do. The web is a rich wellspring of realities, measurements, and figures that can help gigantically.

Obviously, gathering data is just a single piece of doing research for exchanging purposes. The genuine aptitude is in comprehending what data to search for and afterward realizing how to decipher it. This is an ability in itself, yet it's an expertise that can be effortlessly evolved after some time with a lot of training.

In the event that you are set up to commit a not too bad measure of time to doing research and breaking down what you discover then you truly will give yourself a greatly improved possibility of progress with regards to finding conceivably beneficial chances.

## 3. Central and Technical Analysis

Central investigation and specialized examination are the two principle strategies utilized by speculators and brokers to break down data and help figure out what exchanges and ventures to make. In spite of the fact that they are both basically utilized for a similar reason, they are altogether different in the manner in which they are utilized.

Essential examination is fundamentally about gathering however much data as could reasonably be expected identifying with a particular security and afterward dissecting that data to decide the genuine estimation of that security and how it identifies with its exchanging cost.

For instance, on the off chance that you need to do central investigation on a stock in a specific organization, at that point you would consider various parts of that organization, for example, their current money related quality, their profit reports, the nature of their administration work force, and their serious edge in the commercial center. By doing this, you could get a thought of whether the stock was underestimated, exaggerated, or estimated directly comparable to its actual worth. This is to some degree improved, yet it gives you a thought of how essential investigation is utilized.

Specialized investigation is based around utilizing past information to foresee future developments. It includes considering and dissecting outlines and diagrams delineating cost and volume, with the end goal of discovering designs that could uncover patterns that are probably going to be rehashed. The hypothesis is that by following those patterns you can make precise estimates about how a security is going to move in cost over a given period time. Once more, this is a genuinely streamlined perspective on specialized examination, yet it's a sensible outline of what is included.

Both basic examination and specialized investigation are commonly utilized by speculators in stocks, however they have their utilization in alternatives exchanging as well. The general thought is that you would utilize these strategies to assist you with getting a thought of how you would anticipate that the cost of money related instruments should move, and afterward exchange the fitting alternatives agreements to profit by those moves.

Neither principal investigation nor specialized examination can truly be viewed as better than the other one as there are various variables to consider. Somewhat it boils down to individual inclination; in the event that you feel increasingly good utilizing one of the procedures for your examination, or have a specific fitness for it, at that point it clearly bodes well to utilize that strategy. You may like to utilize a mix of both, or utilize key investigation in certain conditions and specialized examination in others.

It merits nothing, however, that choices exchanging is frequently about exploiting transient value developments as opposed to whatever else. Crucial examination can assist you with increasing a comprehension of the innate worth of a security, and it is usually utilized by long haul financial specialists to put resources into underestimated stocks that ought to go up in cost after some time. Be that as it may, it doesn't really assist you with foreseeing value developments in the prompt term.

Specialized examination can, which is the reason choices dealers are most likely bound to profit by utilizing specialized investigation: especially those utilizing a day exchanging style and making a few transient exchanges regularly.

Something else to consider when you are recognizing potential exchanges is how much capital is required and how much hazard is included. Dealing with your spending plan and your introduction to hazard is a significant piece of alternatives exchanging.

**HAZARD AND MONEY MANAGEMENT**

Great administration of your introduction to chance and your exchanging capital is totally crucial in any type of exchanging on the off chance that you can bring in cash over the long haul. There are various techniques you can use for overseeing hazard and controlling your spending plan, for example, utilizing choices spreads and position estimating; our article on hazard and cash the board covers a few of the best ones. We additionally offer guidance on the most proficient method to utilize them.

Effectively dealing with your capital and hazard introduction is basic when exchanging choices. While chance is basically unavoidable with any type of venture, your introduction to chance doesn't need to be an issue. The key is to deal with the hazard reserves viably; consistently guarantee that you are OK with the degree of hazard being taken and that you aren't presenting yourself to unreasonable misfortunes.

Similar ideas can be applied while dealing with your cash as well. You ought to exchange utilizing capital that you can stand to lose; abstain from overstretching yourself. As powerful hazard and cash the board is totally essential to fruitful choices exchanging, it's a subject that you truly need to comprehend. On this page we take a gander at a portion of the techniques you can, and should, use for dealing with your hazard presentation and controlling your spending plan.

1. Utilizing Your Trading Plan

2. Overseeing Risk with Options Spreads

3. Overseeing Risk through Diversification

4. Overseeing Risk utilizing Options Orders

5. Cash Management and Position Sizing

## 1. Utilizing Your Trading Plan

It's critical to have a nitty gritty exchanging plan that spreads out rules and parameters for your exchanging exercises. One of the reasonable employments of such an arrangement is to assist you with dealing with your cash and your hazard introduction. Your arrangement ought to incorporate subtleties of what level of hazard you are alright with and the measure of capital you need to utilize.

By following your arrangement and just utilizing cash that you have explicitly designated for choices exchanging, you can maintain a strategic distance from probably the greatest error that financial specialists and merchants make: utilizing "terrified" cash.

At the point when you are exchanging with cash that you either can't bear to lose or ought to have saved for different purposes, you are far more averse to settle on discerning choices in your exchanges. While it's hard to totally evacuate the feeling engaged with alternatives exchanging, you truly need to be as centered as conceivable around what you are doing and why.

When feeling assumes control over, you conceivably begin to lose your concentration and are at risk to act unreasonably. It might make you pursue misfortunes from past exchanges turned sour, for instance, or making exchanges that you wouldn't normally make. In the event that you follow your arrangement, and stick to utilizing your speculation capital then you should have a greatly improved potential for success of monitoring your feelings.

Similarly, you should hold fast to the degrees of hazard that you layout in your arrangement. On the off chance that you want to make okay exchanges, at that point there truly is no motivation behind why you should begin presenting yourself to more elevated levels of hazard. It's regularly enticing to do this, maybe in light of the fact that you have made a couple of misfortunes and you need to attempt to fix them, or perhaps you have done well with some okay exchanges and need to begin expanding your benefits at a quicker rate.

Be that as it may, on the off chance that you wanted to make generally safe exchanges, at that point you clearly did as such for an explanation, and there is no reason for removing yourself from your customary range of familiarity in view of the equivalent enthusiastic reasons referenced previously.

## 2. Overseeing Risk with Options Spreads

Alternatives spreads are significant and integral assets in choices exchanging. A choices spread is fundamentally when you consolidate more than one situation on choices contracts dependent on the equivalent basic security to adequately make one in general exchanging position.

For instance, on the off chance that you purchased in the cash approaches a particular stock and, at that point worked less expensive out of the cash approaches a similar stock, at that point you would have made a spread known as a bull call spread. Purchasing the calls implies you remain to pick up if the fundamental stock goes up in esteem, yet you would lose a few or the entirety of the cash spent to get them if the cost of the stock neglected to go up. By composing approaches a similar stock you would have the option to control a portion of the underlying expenses and in this manner lessen the most extreme measure of cash you could lose.

All choices exchanging techniques include the utilization of spreads, and these spreads speak to a valuable method to oversee chance. You can utilize them to diminish the forthright expenses of entering a position and to limit how much cash you remain to lose, likewise with the bull call spread model given previously. This implies you possibly diminish the benefits you would make, however it decreases the general hazard.

Spreads can likewise be utilized to diminish the dangers included when entering a short position. For instance, in the event that you wrote in the cash puts on a stock, at that point you would get a forthright installment for composing those choices, however you would be presented to potential misfortunes if the stock declined in esteem. In the event that you likewise purchased less expensive out of cash puts, at that point you would need to invest a portion of your forthright installment, however you would top any potential misfortunes that a decrease in the stock would cause. This specific kind of spread is known as a bull put spread.

As should be obvious from both these models, it's conceivable to enter positions where you despite everything stand to pick up if the value moves the correct route for you, however you can carefully constrain any misfortunes you may bring about if the value moves against you. This is the reason spreads are so generally utilized by alternatives merchants; they are incredible gadgets for hazard the executives.

There is a huge scope of spreads that can be utilized to exploit essentially any economic situation.

**3. Overseeing Risk Through Diversification**

Expansion is a hazard the executives procedure that is normally utilized by financial specialists that are building an arrangement of stocks by utilizing a purchase and hold methodology. The fundamental standard of expansion for such financial specialists is that spreading speculations over various organizations and segments makes a fair portfolio instead of having a lot of cash tied up in one specific organization or part. A differentiated portfolio is commonly viewed as less presented to chance than a portfolio that is made up to a great extent of one explicit kind of venture.

With regards to choices, broadening isn't significant in an incredible same way; anyway it does at present have its uses and you can really expand in various manners. Despite the fact that the standard to a great extent continues as before, you don't need a lot of your capital focused on one specific type of venture, broadening is utilized in choices exchanging through an assortment of techniques.

You can enhance by utilizing a choice of various procedures, by exchanging alternatives that depend on a scope of basic protections, and by exchanging various kinds of choices. Basically, utilizing broadening is that you remain to make benefits in various manners and you aren't totally dependent on one specific result for every one of your exchanges to be fruitful.

## 4. Overseeing Risk Using Options Orders

A moderately straightforward approach to oversee hazard is to use the scope of various requests that you can put. Notwithstanding the four primary request types that you use to open and close situations, there are some of extra requests that you can place, and a considerable lot of these can assist you with hazard the executives.

For instance, an ordinary market request will be filled at the best accessible cost at the hour of execution. This is a flawlessly ordinary approach to purchase and sell choices, yet in an unpredictable market your request may wind up getting filled at a value that is higher or lower than you need it to be. By utilizing limit orders, where you can set least and greatest costs at which your request can be filled, you can abstain from purchasing or selling at less good costs.

There are additionally arranges that you can use to robotize leaving a position: regardless of whether that is to secure benefit previously made or to cut misfortunes on an exchange that has not turned out to be well. By utilizing requests, for example, the cutoff stop request, the market stop request, or the trailing stop request, you can without much of a stretch control when you leave a position.

This will assist you with maintaining a strategic distance from situations where you pass up benefits through clutching a situation for a really long time, or cause large misfortunes by not finishing off on an awful position rapidly enough. By utilizing choices arranges suitably, you can confine the hazard you are presented to on every single exchange you make.

## 5. Cash Management and Position Sizing

Dealing with your cash is inseparably connected to overseeing hazard and both are similarly significant. You at last have a limited measure of cash to utilize, and as a result of this current it's essential to keep a tight control of your capital spending plan and to ensure that you don't lose everything and get yourself unfit to make further exchanges.

The absolute most ideal approach to deal with your cash is to utilize a genuinely straightforward idea known as position estimating. Position estimating is fundamentally choosing the amount of your capital you need to use to enter a specific position.

So as to successfully utilize position measuring, you have to think about the amount to put resources into every individual exchange terms of a level of your general venture capital. In numerous regards, position estimating is a type of expansion. By just utilizing a little level of your capital in any one exchange, you will never be excessively dependent on one explicit result. Indeed, even the best merchants will make exchanges that divert out severely every now and then; the key is to guarantee that the terrible ones don't influence you too seriously.

For instance, in the event that you have half of your venture capital tied up in one exchange and it winds up losing you cash, at that point you will have most likely lost a lot of your accessible assets. In the event that you watch out for just utilize 5% to 10% of your capital per exchange, at that point even a couple of back to back losing exchanges shouldn't clear you out.

On the off chance that you are sure that your exchanging plan will be fruitful over the long haul, at that point you should have the option to get past the terrible periods and still have enough money to make something happen. Position measuring will assist you with doing precisely that.

## ARRANGING INDIVIDUAL TRADES

Our article on arranging singular choices exchanges is basically about assembling all that you have adapted so far to really put in your requests and make your exchanges. We give subtleties of the different advances included, for example, setting your objectives for an exchange and picking which exchanging systems to utilize. We likewise go over the various ways you can leave your exchanges once you have entered them.

So far in our manual for beginning with alternatives exchanging, we have secured various stages you ought to experience when first setting out. We have clarified the significance of being appropriately arranged, gave subtleties to what your readiness ought to include, gave data on picking an online alternatives dealer, and clarified the hugeness of record exchanging levels. We have likewise itemized how to recognize exchanging openings and the strategies you can use to deal with your cash and your introduction to chance.

Expecting that you have absorbed and seen the entirety of the above mentioned, you ought to be prepared to really start purchasing and selling choices. All you have to realize now is the manner by which to assemble all that you have learned and choose which exchanges to make. On this page, we have given a bit by bit process for arranging every individual exchange you make. After some time, this procedure will turn out to be natural to you, and you may even alter it to suit your own inclinations. While you are beginning we suggest you follow the means in the request proposed beneath.

1. Make your Forecast

2. Set your Targets

3. Pick a Strategy

4. Decide Position Size

5. Plan your Entry

6. Set up your Exit

## 1. Make Your Forecast

When you have completed the fundamental research and featured a chance to make an exchange, you have to decide how you are going to attempt to make an arrival. This fundamentally implies choosing what your figure, or standpoint, is on the security you have recognized as a chance.

In the event that you were putting resources into stocks, at that point you would be searching for either stocks that were probably going to increment in esteem so you could get them and benefit from the expansion, or stocks that were probably going to diminish in esteem with the goal that you could short sell them and benefit from the fall. In any case, with choices there are a few unique viewpoints that you can benefit from. You can positively make choices exchanges where you can benefit from a security essentially going up in cost, or from a security going down in cost, yet you can likewise benefit from different situations as well.

For instance, on the off chance that you featured a security that you felt was probably going to stay at its present cost for some time then there are methodologies you could use to profit by that soundness. In the event that you featured a security that you felt would change modestly over some undefined time frame, yet you weren't totally certain whether it would go somewhat up in cost or down in value, at that point there are additionally methodologies where you could make a benefit out of moderate moves in either course.

This is one of the significant advantages of alternatives; regardless of what your attitude toward some random security there is consistently a procedure you can use to attempt to benefit from your conjecture. On the off chance that you are sure that you have accurately determined what will happen to that security, at that point you essentially need to choose a reasonable system, choose the amount to contribute the exchange, and afterward put in the suitable requests. Prior to that, however, you will need to think about setting a few targets.

## 2. Set your Targets

While this is certainly not a vital advance for each exchange you make, it's generally a smart thought to set targets. The fundamental objective you ought to set is how much benefit you wish to make on the grounds that, without realizing the amount you are hoping to make it's difficult to check whether an exchange has been fruitful.

Another objective may be the time allotment wherein you hope to make a specific measure of benefit. This can assist you with spending control since, you might not have any desire to have subsidizes tied up in any one exchange for a really long time. The setting of targets will likewise help you with a portion of the later strides in arranging your exchanges which we spread underneath.

## 3. Pick a Strategy

There are practically boundless ways that you can join different choices positions to attempt to benefit from any standpoint you have on a specific security. The way to progress is truly as basic as utilizing the correct blend at the ideal time. At whatever point you consolidate numerous alternatives positions on the equivalent fundamental security you make choices spreads, and every particular spread is adequately its own interesting methodology. When you have caused a figure on how you to anticipate that the cost of a security should move, you have to choose a system that is correct dependent on what your viewpoint is and any objectives you have set.

For a moderately direct approach to pick a proper exchanging methodology, we would propose investigating our segment devoted to Options Trading Strategies. In this area we have given a complete rundown of the vast majority of the standard procedures that can be utilized. To make it as simple as feasible for you, we have separated these techniques into various classifications. The four primary classifications depend on what viewpoint the methodologies are reasonable for and there are as per the following:

- Bullish Strategies

- Bearish Strategies

- Strategies for a Neutral Market

- Strategies for a Volatile Market

In the event that you visit the pertinent classification, at that point you will see a rundown of techniques that you can use to attempt to cause a benefit from showcase developments you to have determined. A portion of the procedures are moderately straightforward while others are altogether increasingly mind boggling; you simply need to conclude which is the most appropriate for the specific exchange.

Now you should consider chance administration, counseling your exchanging plan if fundamental, and guaranteeing that you are taking a suitable degree of hazard. As you acquire understanding and become increasingly acquainted with all the various techniques, you ought to have the option to settle on a reasonable procedure no sweat. You may likewise think that it is helpful to utilize the accompanying – Selection Tool for Options Trading Strategies.

## 4. Decide Position Size

When you have picked which procedure you will utilize, the subsequent stage is to estimate your position and choose the amount of your capital you will chance. Continuously recollect how significant position estimating is for controlling your financial plan. Regardless of how certain you are that an exchange will be effective, you should restrict the level of your capital that is on the line. Position measuring isn't just about how much cash you are paying at the purpose of making an exchange, but on the other hand it's about how much cash you are putting in danger.

On the off chance that you are making credit spreads for instance, you will get a forthright installment when making the exchange, yet you will be presented to potential future misfortunes. Your potential misfortunes must be considered when you are settling on what level to estimate your position beause, this is eventually the amount of your capital is in danger. Getting this progression wrong might prompt misfortunes that devastate your speculation capital, so compelling position measuring truly is indispensable. Your position estimating ought to likewise consider any objectives you have set.

## 5. Plan your Entry

With the entirety of the above advances finished, you are presently all set ahead and plan your entrance into the pertinent alternatives position. Contingent upon the idea of the open door you have recognized, you may need to trust that specific models will be met before really making the fundamental transactions, or you may need to act right away.

For instance, you may have recognized a security that you contemplate to rise drastically in cost, however you first need affirmation of it arriving at a specific value point or obstruction level. In the event that it doesn't arrive at the necessary level, at that point you don't make the exchange. In the event that it does, at that point you will need to make the exchange as fast as conceivable which is the reason you have to have completed the above advances first. On the off chance that the open door requires prompt activity, at that point you clearly will need to feel free to enter the position as needs be.

To really enter the position and make the exchange, you should put in the fundamental request, or requests, with your representative. It's consistently a smart thought to have a few assets stored with your agent so you can put arranges immediately when you have to. A postponement in putting in your request since you initially need to add a few assets to your record could wind up costing you cash or even outcome in passing up on the chance totally.

In the event that different requests are required, at that point you should choose whether you are going to attempt to have each one of those requests filled all the while or use legging to fill them in stages. When your request is put and your exchange is in progress, at that point you simply have one more advance to consider.

## 6. Set up your Exit

At the purpose of entering a position, you should as of now be contemplating how and when you will be leaving that position. There are various contemplations here, for example, regardless of whether you are wanting to let your positions run until termination or whether you are intending to close them early.

On the off chance that you have set focuses for an exchange, at that point you ought to likewise get ready for shutting your positions on the off chance that you make the necessary degree of benefits or if the predetermined measure of time passes. On the off chance that it comprises of numerous positions, you ought to likewise choose whether you will be shutting all the positions at the same time or legging out of them exclusively. You may likewise need to design when you will cut your misfortunes if things don't work out as expected.

Considering the above data, you should then choose how you will approach shutting your positions when fundamental; there are basically two different ways you can do this. You can either screen the business sectors, shutting the positions when everything looks good, or you can set up programmed leave focuses where conceivable, by utilizing stop arranges for instance. When your exit is readied, you ought to be prepared to proceed onward to your next exchange.